Presents

100 gift
ideas to make
at home

Presents

100 gift ideas to make at home

DAVID & CHARLES
Newton Abbot   London   North Pomfret (Vt)

British Library Cataloguing in Publication Data

Presents.
  1. Handicraft
  I. Darlaston, Pam
  745.5   TT155

  ISBN 0-7153-8213-6

Colour photography by Tony Griffiths LIIP,
Jerome Dessain & Co Ltd
Line illustrations by Linda Coultas

© David & Charles Ltd 1982

First published 1982
Second impression 1983

Typeset by Typesetters (Birmingham) Ltd
and printed in Great Britain
by Butler and Tanner Ltd, Frome
for David & Charles (Publishers) Limited
Brunel House Newton Abbot Devon

Published in the United States of America
by David & Charles Inc
North Pomfret Vermont 05053 USA

CONTENTS

Introduction   7

Patchwork and Appliqué   10
Somerset Patchwork Mats · Petal Cushion · Patchwork
Lampshade · Photograph Frames · Hexagonal Box · Landscape
Panel Cushion · Pram, Bedroom or Cushion Set · Patchwork
Placemat

Soft Toys   21
Murphy the Mouse · McMouse · Terry Turtle · Elephant ·
Charlie the Christmas Mouse · Bumble Bee and Ladybird ·
Lamb Stool · Rabbit · Nursery Book · Penguin · Buzz Bee

Wall Hangings   46
Jute Hanging · Dried Flower Picture · Shell Calendar ·
Three-Dimensional Découpage · Poster Collage · Wild Oat
Marquetry · Choco the Clown · Little Girl Collage

Puppets   55
Nursery Rhyme Finger Puppets · Spider Glove Puppet ·
Sleeping Beauty's Castle · Baby Hand Puppet · Roland the
Rat · Snowman and Clown

Dolls   73
Penelope · Bustle Doll · Queenie Wood · Nightdress Case
Doll · Lavender Handkerchief Doll · Beanbag Mermaid ·
Granny Doll · Lucy Lavender · Mini Doll · Pocket Polly ·
Macramé Bead Dolls

Presents with a Purpose   93
Chicken Egg Cosy · Cat and Mouse Writing Case · Book and
Toy Holder · Potato-Print Apron · Needlepoint Pincushion ·
Bath-Time Panda and His Cuddly Twin · Sweet-Scented
Pincushion · Knitting Needle Case · A Storytime Cushion ·
Miss Pinn

For Children to Make   **112**
Draughts and Chess Set · Shell Vase · Sweet Jar · Lavender
Trinket Box · Christmas Tree Decoration · Mr Rainbow ·
Felt Pencil Tops · Collage Apron · Toy Boat · Teddy Bear
Wall Hanging · Teddy Bookmark · Felt Needlecases ·
Gingerbread Boy

For the Christmas Tree   **120**
Cotton Mould Figures · Furry Fob Key Ring · Christmas
Robin · Cotton Reel Man · Hedgehog and Baby · Mobiles
and Christmas Decorations · Crochet Lavender Hat · Bookworm
Bookmark · Eggshell Decoration · Pressed Flower Miniatures ·
Hetty the Hallowe'en Witch · Mouse Bookmark · Father
Christmas Tree Decoration · Bugs · Dancing Danny · Pressed
Flower Bookmarks, Prayer Bookmarks and Gift Tags

Bags   **132**
Picture Bag · Gift Bags · Needlepoint Purse · Dolly Cocoon ·
Playmat/Toy Bag · Ooloo the Owl · Travel Handy

INTRODUCTION

Lost for ideas for presents? Here are dozens and dozens –
something to suit everyone and to suit every occasion.
You have the opportunity to try your hand at a new
craft; macramé, patchwork, appliqué, découpage and
crochet are represented as well as everyday needlework
skills. There are dolls, soft toys, puppets, cushions,
various wall hangings; there are useful gifts too – a
writing case, pincushions, an assortment of bags, a pram
set, a lampshade and lots of items which could easily be
tackled by children.

There is double pleasure here, both in making a
present and in giving it to someone special, and some of
the gifts will make ideal fundraisers for fêtes and
charities.

Abbreviations and stitches used

Crochet
ch   chain
dc   double crochet
ss   slip stitch
tr   treble crochet

Knitting

k	knit	inc	increased (work into front and back of stitch)
p	purl		
st	stitch		
sts	stitches	dec	decrease (knit 2 stitches together)
tog	together		
DK	double knitting yarn	LSLW	leave sewing length of wool
		st st	stocking stitch

moss stitch: k1, p1, k1, p1 etc rows 1, 3, 5 etc
            p1, k1, p1, k1 etc rows 2, 4, 6 etc

stocking stitch: k rows 1, 3, 5 etc
                p rows 2, 4, 6 etc

Embroidery

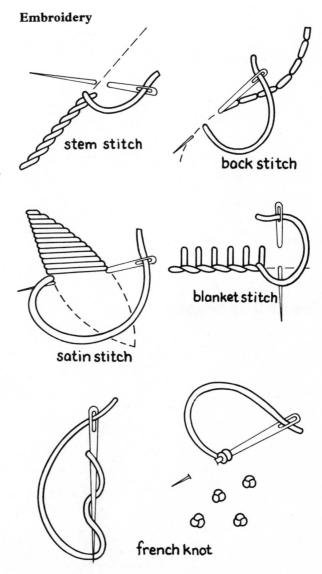

stem stitch

back stitch

satin stitch

blanket stitch

french knot

Needlepoint

Tramming (long staggered horizontal stitches) is worked over canvas before other stitching to help cover the threads or to give padding.

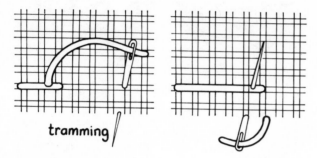

tramming

Macramé

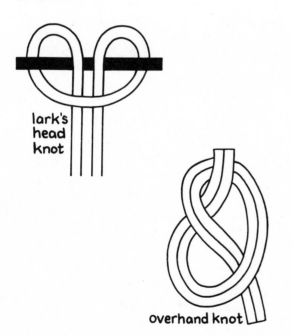

lark's head knot

overhand knot

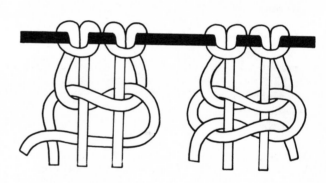

square (flat) knot

8

Transferring patterns

A design can be transferred to fabric in a number of ways.

1 Using a washable transfer pencil or tailor's pencil, draw directly on to the fabric round templates, etc.

2 Tack paper or card shapes into position. Tack round them, outlining the shapes, then remove the papers.

3 Pin and tack paper pattern to fabric, cut round edges.

4 Place dressmaker's carbon (available in different colours) between the fabric and design and draw over the outlines with a sharp pencil. Make sure that the fabric, carbon and design are firmly anchored.

5 A special transfer pencil can be used to trace the design, which is then ironed on to the fabric. In most cases, the design will be reversed.

Enlarging patterns

1 Trace the outline from the book on to tracing paper.

2 Rule a grid of squares all over. Number the squares.

3 Take a sheet of paper the final size required and rule a grid of squares all over, the same number of squares as the first grid. Number the squares.

4 Draw in the design, carefully copying whatever is in each square of the small grid to the corresponding larger square. Use a dark felt pen or ink so that the enlarged outline can be easily traced and transferred to fabric.

Stuffings and glues

Various stuffings are available – kapok, foam chips, polystyrene granules, old tights. The stuffing chosen must depend on the present and its use, whether it is to be washable, whether a smooth finish is required, etc. Care must be taken to use the correct glue for the materials you are working with. Read the instructions on the tube carefully – for example, some glues can dissolve polystyrene.

Safety

Particular care should be taken when making presents for babies and young children. Washable fabrics are desirable, felt eyes are safest but if 'real' eyes are preferred, use special safety eyes. Avoid sharp edges and make sure that everything is sewn on securely. Paints used for children's gifts must be non-toxic.

Somerset Patchwork Mats
Madeleine Howard, Chelmsford

A striking sextet of placemats, cleverly made using the folded technique of 'Somerset patchwork'. The mats, 18.5cm in diameter, are easy to make and great fun can be had working out suitable colour combinations. By using a larger foundation circle and increasing the number of segments, the pattern can be adapted to make a cushion.

Materials (for 6 mats)
60×40cm piece of sheeting
oddments of 6 contrasting or toning cottons – prints or plain
  for each mat
60×40cm lining material
bias binding

Method
1 Draw round a 19cm diameter soup plate or similar using a biro or marking pen on the piece of sheeting.

2 Cut around on the line. Fold each circle in half and then in quarters and press the folds in. Open out and the exact middle will be evident.

3 Choose a colour for the middle of the mat and cut out 4 circles 7.5cm in diameter. It is helpful to draw round a cup of the appropriate size on to a piece of thin card and then use that as a template.

4 Fold the material circles in half, then fold the edges in to the middle (a), to form a 'segment' shape. Press with an iron and a little spray starch to keep the 'segment' shape crisp.

5 Place these four, with the points facing inwards, touching the centre of the foundation circle (b).

6 Attach the points to the centre of the foundation circle by hand with a few oversewn stitches which will lose themselves in the point.

7 Stitch around the outer edges, either with a firm running stitch or use a machine stitch, about 3mm in from the segment edges.

8 Prepare 8 more circles, of a toning or contrasting

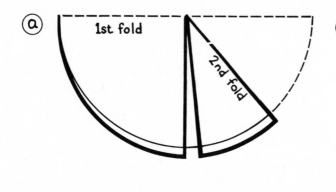

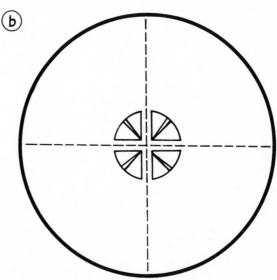

colour, in exactly the same way and position them so that the points are in line with the points of the first 4 segments and about 20mm from the centre. Stitch as before.

9 Continue with 3 more rows. In the last row it may be necessary to finish with 16 segments in order to cover the final raw edges and previous stitching.

10 Line with a suitable material, putting in more padding if necessary. Finish the edge with bias binding in a matching or contrasting colour.

Petal Cushion
Jo Watson, Ilkley, West Yorks

An unusual cushion in shades of blue which really does look like a series of petals. The cushion is 40cm in diameter.

Materials
2 circles of toning or contrasting fabric, 40cm diameter, to make cushion cover
40cm diameter cushion pad
pieces of blue-coloured fabrics – plain and patterned
10cm square of card
8cm diameter circle of thin foam

Method
1 Cut a 10cm square template out of card.
2 Using the template draw round and cut out squares from oddments of material. You will need 150–170 10cm squares.
3 Fold each square in half diagonally then fold the two points A and C down to B (a).
4 Stitch from D to E and cut off the bottom corner (b).
5 Pin a circle of triangles around the cushion cover about 3.5cm from the edge, each triangle overlapping the middle of the next. Stitch in place.
6 Stitch the next round so that the previous stitches are hidden.
7 Continue in this way until a 7.5–10cm circle remains. As you get nearer to the centre it will be

necessary to run a strong thread around to gather the petals slightly.

8 To make the flower centre cut out a 10cm circle of material. Run gathering stitches round the edge and draw up slightly. Pad with 8cm circle of thin foam. Stitch into position.

9 To finish, with right sides together, carefully tack then sew backing on to petal front, being careful not to stitch petals, leaving a 15cm opening to turn. Put cushion pad inside and slip stitch opening.

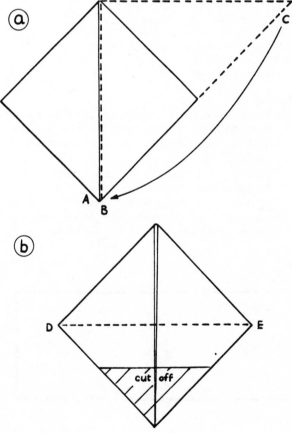

11

Patchwork Lampshade

Kathleen Embrey, Shrewsbury

Here patchwork is sewn with a zig-zag stitch to make this attractive lampshade.

Materials
2 lampshade rings 22.5cm diameter
2.25m soft lampshade tape, white
73×20cm iron-on Vilene
72.5×20cm Selabond card (used for making firm lampshades)
plain and patterned cotton material
1.8m nylon velvet ribbon to tone
UHU glue
clothes pegs for holding to ring while stitching
strong white cotton
diamond template, size as shown

Method
1   Using the template, cut out 45 patterned and 40 plain diamonds in cotton material. The diamonds must be cut exactly to size with no overlap or turnings.
2   Draw pencil lines across the centre of the Vilene, horizontally and vertically.
3   Starting at the centre with a patterned diamond, place one long row along the centre line, just touching each one with the tip of a hot iron.

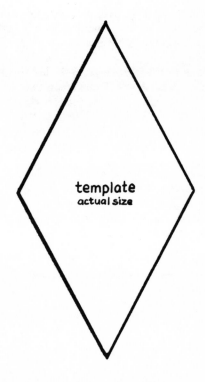

template
actual size

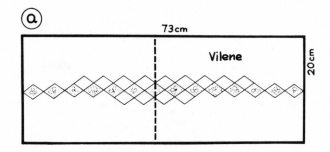

4   Follow with a row of plain diamonds above and below (a), and continue in this way until all the Vilene is covered. Iron again.
5   Select a fancy zig-zag stitch and machine over the raw edges.
6   Place the patchwork on the Selabond and smooth over, leaving the surplus 5mm overlap free at one end.
7   Carefully bind the lampshade rings with the tape, taking care to just overlap.
8   Secure the card to the rings with pegs, and then stitch firmly in place. Overlap the seam and join with glue.
9   Attach ribbon trim to top and bottom.

Photograph Frames
Barbara Baines, Ponteland, Northumberland

Designed to match the hexagonal box on page 14, these frames will look charming on the dressing table or mantelpiece.

Materials
4 pieces stiff card 17.5×21cm
2 pieces acetate sheet 20×16cm
2 pieces of thin wadding 18×21.5cm
40×26cm printed fabric
40×26cm plain fabric
PVA glue
matching thread
handyknife
cutting board
flat-bladed knife to spread glue

Method
1   Cut 4 pieces of card to size. Trace ovals on 2 pieces and cut out centre with handyknife. Stick wadding to fronts and cut out oval holes.
2   Cut printed fabric to fit fronts with 1cm turnings.
3   Using flat-bladed knife apply 1cm of PVA glue round outside edges of back of the cards with holes. Cover with fabric and iron over glued edges. Cut out centre of fabric leaving 15mm for turnings. Snip all round. Glue and iron into place.
4   Glue 5mm turning along two long edges of plain fabric. Position back cards to allow for thickness of fronts, leaving about 15mm between cards for 'hinge'. Glue and iron turnings on to cards.
5   Position fronts and sew in place round three outer sides leaving central edges free to insert acetate sheet and photographs.

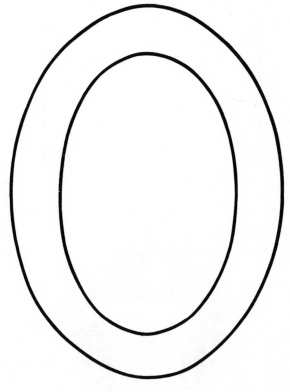

enlarge × 1½

13

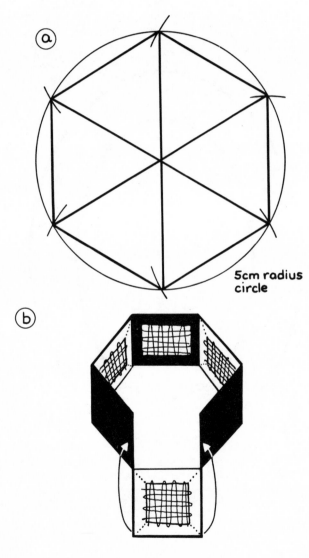

(a)

5cm radius
circle

(b)

Hexagonal Box
Barbara Baines, Ponteland, Northumberland

This unusual box provides a delightful place to store one's treasures. Beautifully worked and finished, it is surprisingly simple and inexpensive to make. It measures 10.5cm wide × 4cm deep.

Materials
heavy card
thin card
scraps of cotton fabric
matching thread (polyester)
crochet thread or cord to trim lid

Method
1 To make a hexagon, using compasses, draw a 5cm radius circle. Mark off 6 equidistant points on the circumference. Join up and draw in diameters to form 6 triangles (a).
2 Cut 2 hexagons in heavy card and 2 in thin card. Cut 1 heavy hexagon into triangles. Cut 6 rectangles 5 × 4cm in heavy card and 6 rectangles in thin card to the same size.
3 From two toning fabrics (one print and one plain, using plain for lining) cut – with 1cm allowance all round – 3 triangles and 3 rectangles in printed cotton, and 3 triangles, 9 rectangles and 3 hexagons in plain cotton.
4 Using heavy card, lace fabric over 6 triangles for lid (take care to make corners neat and firm), 6 rectangles for sides and the hexagon for bottom.
5 Sew the triangles together from the wrong side to form a hexagon with alternating fabrics.
6 Sew alternating rectangles to base hexagon from wrong side, then fold sides up and join rectangles on the right side to form box (b).
7 Lining. Using thin card, lace lining hexagon for inside of lid. Place wrong sides together with made-up triangle. Join round outside edge with double knot stitch (c), or alternatively stitch and sew round a

14

piece of cord leaving a loop at front to lift the lid. Make a loop and buttonhole stitch it.

NB The card shapes for the rest of the lining must be trimmed to fit inside box, allowing for thickness of covering fabric. The amount to be trimmed away will vary with the thickness of cards used, so try them in place carefully before lacing fabric over card.

8 Work as for outer box but join sides on wrong side.

9 Place lining in box. Press down very firmly. Stitch together along top edges. If lid is trimmed with double knot stitch, work a short length of the stitch along top of one rectangular side for hinge and slip-stitch lid in place here. If using cord trim, sew through cord taking care not to catch the lid.

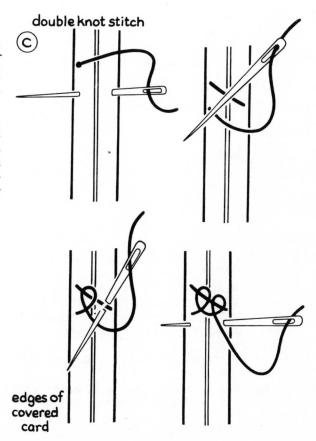

double knot stitch

Ⓒ

edges of covered card

Landscape Panel Cushion
Jean Aucock, Haytor, Devon

The materials have been carefully chosen to blend and contrast and the panel is skilfully finished with embroidered motifs and framed with machined satin stitch. The cushion measures 38 × 38cm.

Materials
40cm cushion pad
2 pieces 40.5 × 40.5cm fabric for back and front cover
32.5 × 32.5cm fabric in contrasting colour
toning fabrics for centre panel picture
matching and contrasting sewing threads
iron-on interfacing

Method
1 Begin with centre panel. Make paper pattern for centre panel by drawing your own design on paper 32.5 × 32.5cm and cutting out each shape.
2 Using this pattern, cut picture pieces from toning fabrics and back with iron-on interfacing. Arrange on 32.5 × 32.5cm fabric piece and tack in place. Using narrow satin stitch, sew picture pieces to backing fabric. Add extra hand or machine embroidery as required.
3 With right sides uppermost, place picture panel over front cover piece and sew around the edge using wide satin stitch. To 'frame' the picture, sew another line of wide satin stitch about 5mm outside the edge of the picture.
4 Place front and back pieces together, right sides facing. Tack, then stitch around three sides, taking 12mm turnings. Stitch about 5cm along each end of the fourth side. Trim corners, turn back and press 12mm along open edges. Turn cover right side out and press. Insert cushion pad and slipstitch along open edge.

Pram, Bedroom or Cushion Set
Avril Dunn, Penzance, Cornwall

This pretty set of covers, made with an opening back, can be as elaborate or as simple as you please – quilted, patchwork, lacy and frilly, ribboned and appliquéd. The set illustrated, a pram quilt and pillow cover, is made in quilted cotton patchwork and is completely washable. Extra warmth is added to the quilt by an inner bag filled with double wadding. The same basic design can also be used as a cushion set, or a bedroom set of daytime pillow cover and nightdress case. The quilt measures 47.5 × 60cm and the pram pillow 35 × 42.5cm (to take a standard-size pram safety pillow).

Materials
50 × 115cm fabric (washable) for front
110 × 115cm cotton for lining and back only, *or*
160 × 115cm cotton for lining, back and inner bag (or use discarded sheets or pillow cases)
1m polyester wadding, cut in single layers
thread to match top fabric and back
10cm Velcro fastening

Method
Cut out fabric following pattern layouts.

Quilt front
1 Take front fabric, wadding (1 piece) and lining of the same size. Pin edges together and baste through all layers at regular intervals. For simple quilting, use the quilting foot on the machine and quilt from the front, in a diamond, square or line pattern. For more elaborate quilting draw a pattern on the lining before basting and quilt from the back. In the set illustrated, a diamond-shaped design of simple patchwork has been zig-zag stitched to the front cover after quilting.
2 Add lace, ribbon or other trimming.
3 Remove basting cotton carefully.
To make a simpler cover, omit the wadding and quilting.

16

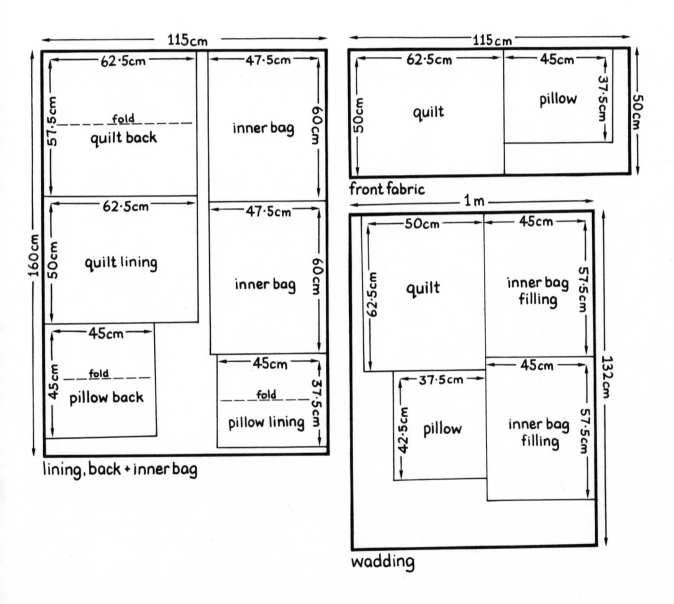

115cm

62·5cm

57·5cm

fold
quilt back

50cm

62·5cm

quilt lining

160cm

45cm

fold
pillow back

45cm

47·5cm

inner bag

60cm

47·5cm

inner bag

60cm

45cm

fold
pillow lining

37·5cm

lining, back + inner bag

115cm

62·5cm

quilt

50cm

45cm

pillow

37·5cm

50cm

front fabric

1 m

50cm

quilt

62·5cm

45cm

inner bag filling

57·5cm

37·5cm

pillow

42·5cm

45cm

inner bag filling

57·5cm

132cm

wadding

17

Quilt back

1 Take back fabric, fold in half lengthwise and cut along this fold to give two pieces.
2 Turn back 25mm on two centre edges and make hem for opening.
3 Mark centre point on hems of centre opening.
4 Cut Velcro into 8mm pieces. Sew one piece of velvet-side Velcro to centre point on top of one hem and sew one piece of hook-side Velcro to centre point on underside of other hem. Repeat at 8cm intervals, using 5 pieces of Velcro on each side of the quilt back. Join Velcro, matching hems at the edges, and sew along the hem for 10cm at either end.

Joining front and back

1 Place front and back right sides together. (Hems on back are turned to the wrong side.) Match edges, pin and trim if necessary. Sew all round 12mm from the edge.
2 Trim away excess wadding and neaten corners, taking care not to cut the stitches.
3 Turn right side out, carefully push out corners and edges, and press the edge.
4 Using top thread to match front fabric and bobbin thread to match back, sew again, right side up, 12mm from the edge.
5 Press lightly to finish. Do not press quilting on the right side – only very lightly on the back.

Pillow

Follow exactly the same directions above, but using 3 pieces of Velcro instead of 5.

Inner bag for pram quilt

1 Take 2 pieces of cotton, place right sides together and sew 10mm from the edge round three sides, leaving one short side open.
2 Turn right side out, turn back 5mm to inside of bag on this short side and sew a single hem.
3 Place 2 pieces of wadding together and put into bag, smoothing out and pushing well into corners. Close top of bag by hand stitching the edge.
4 Place this warmer inside quilt cover. (When using in the pram, sew the opening lightly together by hand to prevent baby kicking it open.)

To convert pram set to a cushion or bedroom set

1 Remove inner warmer from quilt and unpick the stitching at the end.
2 Add more wadding or foam chips, re-close bag, and replace in quilt.
3 Remove safety pad from pillow and make a bag size 35×43cm in the same way as for quilt. Fill with foam chips and replace in cover.

To make covers for a larger pillow, measure size of pillow to be used and add 5cm to width and length of size of pillow for front, lining and wadding, and add 10cm to width and 5cm to length for back which is later cut in half lengthwise.

Patchwork Placemat

Mary Belsham, Billingshurst, Sussex

This placemat, made with a patchwork top and an inter-lining of Vilene and wadding, is heatproof and washable. A set can be made by hand or by machine, and requires only small amounts of bright cottons.

Materials (for each 25cm diameter mat)
strong brown paper, for the pattern
50×50cm cotton fabric, for the backing, centre circle and 4 front patches (Material A)
25×25cm cotton fabric in contrasting or toning colour for 4 front patches (Material B)
30×30cm medium-weight, sew-in Vilene, for the patchwork base
40×30cm wadding for the interlining
1.3m ricrac braid in white or matching colour

Method
1 On thick paper draw 2 identical circles with a 12.5cm radius. Mark centres.
2 The first circle is the pattern for the patchwork base, the interlining and the backing. Cut out carefully on the pencil outline and make a hole in the centre with a pencil point.
3 The second circle is for the patchwork top. Draw a circle 2.5cm radius from centre point and divide outer ring into 8 equal segments. Number these and mark each to show the grain of the fabric. Cut out segments and centre circle. Make a hole with pencil point in centre of small circle.
4 Mark fabric on reverse side using a soft pencil; make sure that it does not show through to the right side.
5 Lay first circle on Material A, mark round edge and mark centre. Cut out with 12mm seam allowance.
6 Lay segments 1, 3, 5, 7 on Material A, matching arrows with grain. Mark round edge of each segment and number each piece. Cut out with 12mm seam allowance.

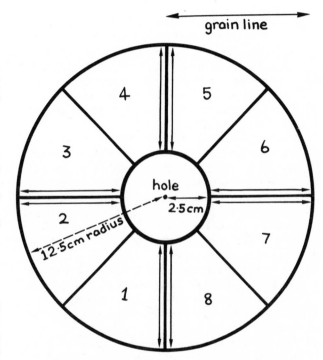

7 Lay small circle for centre on Material A, mark round the edge and cut out with 12mm seam allow-ance. Mark centre.
8 Lay segments 2, 4, 6, 8 on Material B and proceed as for segments above.
9 Make patchwork top by applying segments to Vilene base. For accuracy mark Vilene on both sides. Place patches on right side, but stitch from the reverse, so that slight inaccuracies are not carried forward. Lay first circle on Vilene and draw round. Mark centre. Lay pattern for small circle on this, centres matching, and draw round. Lay segments 1 to 8 on outside ring and rule these off so that markings corre-spond to second circle pattern. It is not necessary to mark grain lines or number segments, but marking

19

should be firm so that it shows through fabric. Turn Vilene over and trace on reverse strengthening outline which should now be the same on both sides. Cut round outer circle, with 12mm seam allowance.

10 Lay first circle and small circle on wadding for interlining and cut out, with 12mm seam allowance.

11 Place segment 1 on Vilene right side up with outlines matching. Pin firmly.

12 Place segment 2 face down on segment 1, with outlines matching. Pin firmly. Turn the Vilene over and sew on left side only through all thicknesses on marked line. Remove pins, and on front, flip segment 2 over on to its right side, press down and pin flat.

13 Lay segment 3 face down on segment 2, matching outlines, pin and sew left side only from back of Vilene. Flip over and press as before. Repeat this until all segments are used.

14 To finish the last segment fold over and press the remaining side under along seam line. Sew down to seam line of patch 1 with invisible stitches.

15 Cut out centre ring of Vilene 6mm inside marked line.

16 The marking of the outer edge of the patchwork top must be brought through to the front. Do this by running round with coloured thread.

17 Tack ricrac braid on front of patchwork round outside ring, with centre of braid on the coloured thread.

18 Tack interlining to reverse of lining.

19 With right sides together and grain lines matching, pin patchwork top to lining and interlining. Stitch together round the outside ring marked by coloured thread. This stitching will go through patchwork, ricrac, lining and interlining.

Trim seam allowance on all thicknesses to 6mm. Remove tacking. Turn mat right side out through centre opening. Press.

20 Transfer marking of outside ring to front of centre patch by coloured thread as before.

21 Pin interlining to inside of patch.

22 Sew ricrac firmly to front of patch and interlining, with centre of braid on coloured thread. Trim interlining to stitching.

23 Turn under seam allowance all round so that only the tips of the ricrac show on the right side. Press.

24 Matching centres, pin centre on top opening. Top stitch through ricrac as close to the edge as possible, stitching through all layers. Press well.

SOFT TOYS *illustrated in colour on pages 26 and 27*

Murphy the Mouse
Linda M. Crooks, Whaley Bridge, Stockport

A simple yet effective soft toy whose size and character (he has orange ears) are larger than life – indeed he is 25cm long and 13cm high. He might even venture along his run to provide an unusual doorstop!

Materials
velvet or dralon
coloured felt (ears and feet)
white felt (eyes)
length of brown cord (tail)
stuffing

enlarge × 3

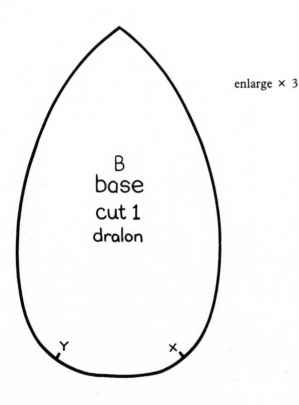

C
ear
cut 4 + sew
into 2 pairs
felt

D
foot
cut 4
felt

A
body
cut 2
dralon

back

sew ear here

foot position

foot position

B
base
cut 1
dralon

Y   X

Method

1 Cut out pattern pieces A and B from dralon.
2 Cut out pattern pieces C and D from felt.
3 Sew ears to body pieces.
4 Wrong sides together, sew body pieces together across back.
5 Sew base to body leaving X-Y open for stuffing, and set in feet.
6 Turn to right side and stuff firmly.
7 Sew across opening and catch tail in centre.
8 Cut out eyes from black and white felt and glue on face.

21

McMouse

Eileen B. Massey, Holbeton, Plymouth

A handsome tartaned gentleman, 28cm high, beautifully made and finished, who somehow manages to combine an immaculate appearance with a cuddly character.

Materials

102×9cm plaid (kilt)
70×11cm plaid (bottom body, base and hat)
46×46cm green fabric (coat)
14×9cm beige fur fabric
20×10cm white fur fabric (ear lining)
scraps of yellow, black and brown felt and long hair fur
28cm cord (tail)
36mm lace 16mm wide (cuffs)
18cm double-edged lace 25mm wide (jabot)
2 small buttons (or felt)
feather (or felt)
1 pair brown safety eyes
1 black safety nose
38cm braid 12mm wide (belt)
stuffing

Method

1 Cut out pattern pieces, reversing where necessary. Turning allowances are included and all seams are made with right sides together.

2 Ears. Join beige and white pieces together, trim, turn and gather ear from A to B. Repeat for second ear.

3 Face. Stitch from C to D and from E to F. Insert nose between D and E, and eyes, securely fitting washers. Join ears to face and ease to fit.

4 Back of Head. Stitch darts and join centre back seam from G to H. Join face to back of head.

5 Arms. Join paws to arms. Join arm pieces together leaving opening where indicated, trim, turn and stuff. Stitch up opening.

6 Cuff. Join short ends of lace and using a running stitch gather cuff to fit wrist and stitch to wrist seam. Repeat for other arm.

7 Feet. Join top of foot to sole making 2 folds where indicated, trim, turn and stuff.

8 Top body. Join centre front seam. Gather lace front and stitch to centre front seam where indicated. Join centre back seam from J to K and then join back to front. Stitch head to body matching centre fronts.

9 Bottom body. Join centre front seam. Join centre back seam inserting tail where indicated. Join side seams. Stitch feet to body where indicated. Insert base. Trim and turn.

10 Kilt. Pull a few threads from both short ends for fringe and make narrow hem. Press. Starting at centre back, fold fabric evenly to give 2cm wide pleats. Press. Wrap over fronts to fit waist and tack to bottom body matching centre fronts and backs. Tack top of body to bottom matching seams and enclosing kilt. Machine and turn.

11 Pin arms to side seams with top of arm in line with neck seam. On inside of body work a circle of back stitches to join arms securely to body. Also on inside catch top of foot to body to stop feet dropping.

12 Stuff toy firmly, taking particular care at nose. Stitch up opening.

13 To finish, sew buttons on very firmly where indicated. Cut a narrow strip of yellow felt and stick around neck for collar. Stick two pieces of yellow felt together, when dry cut out buckle and cut two slits to thread belt through. Stick to body, bottom edge of belt to waist seam. Stick fur sporran to black felt and fold over top of felt and stick to right side of sporran. Stick to kilt immediately beneath buckle.

14 Hat. Stitch top to bottom. Join short ends of hatband. Sew one edge of band to hat, fold over other edge and hem on inside. Place a little stuffing in hat and sew to head. Stitch feather to side of hatband and cover stitching with a half circle of yellow felt.

15 Comb all furry parts and give toy a good brushing to remove all traces of stuffing. Finally add some whiskers by using brown thread and knot firmly to stop them pulling out.

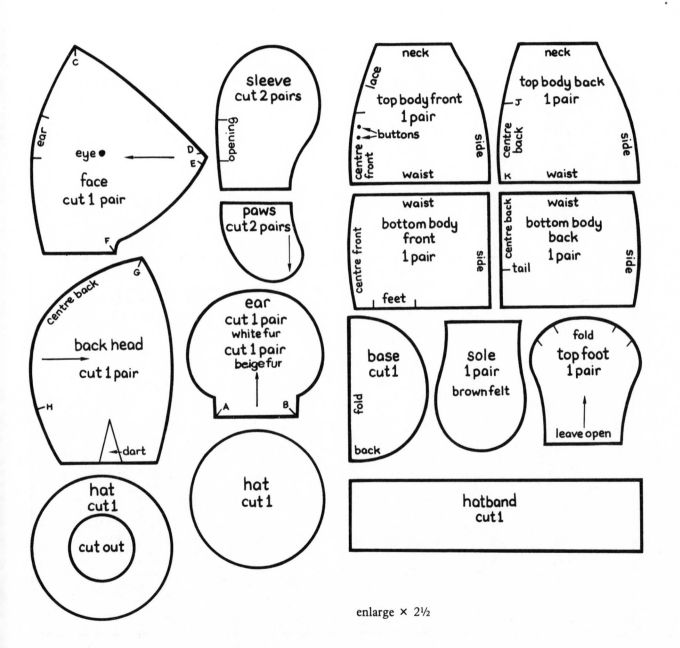

enlarge × 2½

PATCHWORK AND APPLIQUÉ *(opposite)*

1   Landscape Panel Cushion *(page 16)*
2   Patchwork Lampshade *(page 12)*
3   Petal Cushion *(page 11)*
4   Photograph Frames *(page 13)*
5   Hexagonal Box *(page 14)*
6   Patchwork Placemat *(page 19)*
7   Somerset Patchwork Mats *(page 10)*
8   Pram, Bedroom or Cushion Set *(page 16)*

SOFT TOYS *(overleaf)*

1   Lamb Stool *(page 38)*
2   Nursery Book *(page 41)*
3   Buzz Bee *(page 44)*
4   Penguin *(page 42)*
5   Elephant *(page 33)*
6   McMouse *(page 22)*
7   Charlie the Christmas Mouse *(page 33)*
8   Bumble Bee and Ladybird *(page 35)*
9   Rabbit *(page 40)*
10 Murphy the Mouse *(page 21)*
11 Terry Turtle *(page 30)*

CALENDAR

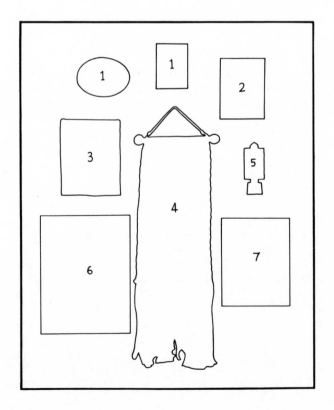

WALL HANGINGS (opposite)

1 Three-Dimensional Découpage *(page 48)*
2 Little Girl Collage *(page 54)*
3 Wild Oat Marquetry *(page 50)*
4 Jute Hanging *(page 46)*
5 Shell Calendar *(page 48)*
6 Poster Collage *(page 50)*
7 Dried Flower Picture *(page 46)*

Terry Turtle
Wendy Gough, London N1

This fine fellow has a body knitted in stocking stitch and a sewn 'shell'. He is easy to make yet most effective.

Materials
35g DK grey
15g DK red
1 pair 3¼mm (No 10) needles
28×24cm beige felt
stuffing
2 ball buttons or felt for eyes
1 button for shell
wool or embroidery thread for mouth and shell

Method
Turtle (front and back both alike)
Leg: in grey cast on 8sts. Then working in st st
Row 1: k
Row 2: inc 1 st, p to end, inc 1 st
Repeat rows 1 and 2 until there are 14sts
Work 3 rows
Next row: dec 1 st at each end of this and alternate rows until there are 8 sts
Work 10 rows
Work next 2 rows in red*
Leave sts on spare needle
Work second leg to * then:

Body
1 Knit across this leg in grey, turn and cast on 24sts, turn and knit across sts on spare needle (40sts).
2 Next row: p, dec 1st at each end of row.
3 Work 2 rows red, 2 rows grey, 2 rows red, dec 1st at each end of every row (26sts).
4 Work 2 rows grey, 2 rows red, then break off red and work 9 rows grey.
5 Inc 1st each end of every row until there are 40sts.
6 Next row: k10, cast off 3, k14 (including st left on needle), cast off 3, k to end.

Leg
7 Working on these 10sts, work 10 rows straight.
8 Next and alternate rows: inc 1st at each end of row (14sts).
9 Work 3 rows straight.
10 Next and alt. rows: dec 1st at each end (10sts).
11 Cast off.

Head
12 Rejoin wool to central 14sts and work 8 rows.
13 Next and alt. rows: inc 1st at each end of row (20sts).
14 Work 10 rows.
15 Next and alt. rows: dec 1st at each end of row (16sts).
16 Cast off.
17 Rejoin wool to last 10sts and complete to match first leg.

Making up
1 Press pieces. Embroider mouth on one piece, sew or embroider eyes on the other.
2 Sew up seams leaving cast-off edges of head open.
3 Turn right side out and stuff firmly, leaving 'joints' of legs slightly less firmly stuffed. Sew up opening.

Shell
1 Cut out pieces A, B and C.
2 Sew B to C along dotted lines.
3 Make 'shell' markings on A as in diagram, using felt-tip pen, chain stitch or machine stitching.
4 Sew round edges of A and B, leaving an opening between a and a, 1cm from the edge.
5 Stuff shell lightly, and stitch up opening.
6 Trim edge of shell with pinking shears. Sew button on to C, and snip buttonhole to fit.

A a a

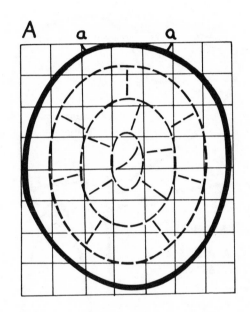

each square
represents
2cm x 2cm

B a a

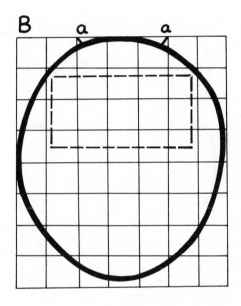

C

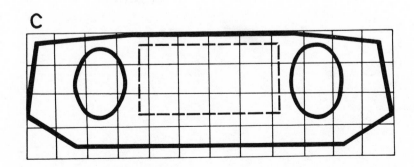

31

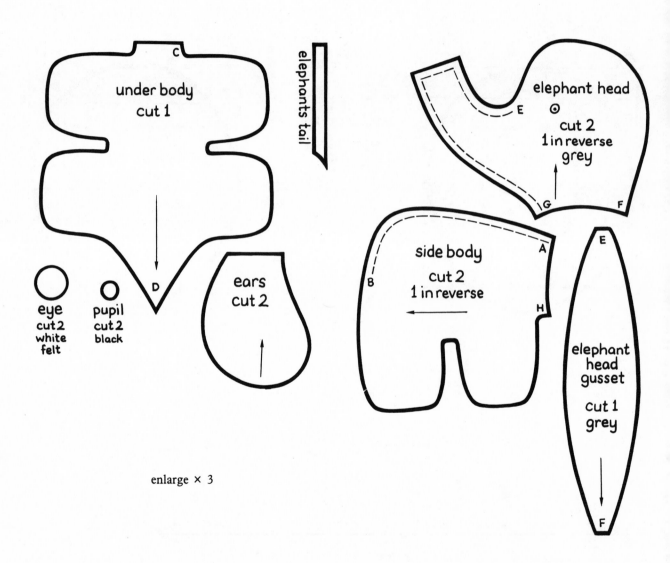

under body
cut 1

C

D

elephants tail

elephant head
cut 2
1 in reverse
grey

E

G

F

eye
cut 2
white
felt

pupil
cut 2
black

ears
cut 2

side body
cut 2
1 in reverse

A

B

H

elephant
head
gusset

cut 1
grey

E

F

enlarge × 3

32

Elephant

Mary J. Younge, Alkrington, Lancs

This simple pattern can be adapted quite easily to make a rabbit or a dog. Made out of furry material and felt, 25cm high, he is suitable for all ages.

Materials
Fur fabric – 0.5m grey
30 × 30cm pink felt for ears
safety eyes (or use black and white felt)
stuffing – kapok or cut-up old tights

Method
Body
1 Cut out 2 side body patterns from grey fur fabric, reversing the pattern before cutting the second piece. Then, with right sides together, sew from A to B.
2 Right sides together, attach underbody to side body by sewing C to D on both sides, easing in the point at the bottom of underbody. Turn inside out.

Head
1 With right sides together sew gusset to side head from E to F, easing round top of head. Do the same with the other side head.
2 Sew sides together from E to G to form the trunk. Turn right side out.
3 Attach head to body and sew across the front.
4 Stuff the head and body carefully, moulding the body into shape. Stuff the neck firmly and sew back of head to body with ladder stitch, stuffing as you work round. It is most important to ensure that the neck is firmly stuffed.
5 Sew nose, eyes and ears in position, sew on tail and tie a ribbon around the neck.

Charlie the Christmas Mouse

Pat Oldham, Rochdale

Charlie Mouse can be used as any kind of mascot – make him in your favourite team colours, small or large. Instead of stuffing the sack, add sweets or a present.

Materials
oddments of DK wool in red, white, black, pink and turquoise
felt for eyes and nose
stuffing
3¼mm (No 10) needles

Method

Body
1 Cast on 40sts in black, knit 6 rows (boots).
2 Change to pink and work 6 rows st st (socks).
3 Knit 22 rows in red (legs).
4 Change to black and work 4 rows in st (belt).
5 Knit 14 rows in red (body).
6 Next row: k6, k2tog, k4, k2tog, k12, k2tog, k4, k2tog, k6 (36sts).
7 Knit 3 rows in red (neck).
8 Change to white and k 2 rows (neck).
9 Next row: k6, inc, k4, inc, k12 inc, k4 inc, k6 (40sts).
10 Knit 20 rows in white (head).
11 Next row: k2tog to end (20sts).
12 Break off wool leaving a long end, run through remaining stitches. When the mouse has been stuffed, this thread can be drawn up tightly and finished off.

Arms
1 Cast on 16 sts in red, k 20 rows.
2 Change to black and work 2 rows in st st.
3 Knit 8 rows in white.
4 Next row: k2tog to end (8sts). Break off wool leaving a long end, run through remaining stitches and draw up tightly.

Nose

1 Cast on 2sts in white, k1 row.
2 Inc 1st at each end of next and every alternate row until there are 24 sts. Cast off.

Ears

Knit 4 pieces: 2 white and 2 pink
1 Cast on 8sts, k1 row.
2 Inc 1st at each of the next row and each alternate row until there are 20sts.
3 Knit 5 rows.
4 K2tog, knit to last 2sts, k2tog.
5 Next row: k.
6 As instruction 4.
7 As instruction 5.

Hat

1 Cast on 20sts in red, knit 8 rows for brim.
2 Cast off 1st at each end of next row and every 4th row until 10sts remain.
3 Cast off.

Tail

Cast on 3sts in white. Knit 40 rows. Cast off.

Scarf

Cast on 5sts in turquoise. Knit 50 rows. Cast off.

Sack

Cast on 15sts in any colour. Knit 20 rows. Cast off.

To make up

1 Join back seam of body and turn right side out.
2 Place lower edge of back seam between 20th and 21st stitches, sew centre front of mouse at lower edge to back seam, continue sewing through mouse at centre position for 5.5cm (2¼in) up body to form legs.
3 Stuff body and head through top of head and stuff legs through lower edge.
4 Pull the wool up tightly at top of head and fasten off,

sew across base of feet.
5 Shape neck by tying length of matching wool tightly round lower edge of head.
6 Nose. Fold in half, join seam. Stuff. Sew on to face. Place a small circle of felt on tip of nose and sew securely.
7 Eyes. Cut out two small round pieces of black felt, sew securely in position.
8 Whiskers. Thread white or black thread through nose and fasten off securely.
9 Ears. Join one white and one pink piece together, slightly gather base of ears and sew to head.
10 Hat. Join seam. Stuff lightly. Turn up brim and attach hat to head between ears. Add a pom-pom to tip of hat.
11 Scarf. Add fringe to cast off edges, and tie round neck.
12 Sack. Fold in half and join the seam. Stuff. Run a thread of wool round top of sack and draw up tying with a bow.
13 Tail. Sew to mouse's bottom.
14 Arms. Join seam. Stuff. Attach to top of body. Place one arm by the mouse's side, the other one in a position to hold sack.

Bumble Bee and Ladybird
Ruth C. Hindley, Worksop, Notts

An unusual and striking duo made out of fur fabric and felt, 25cm high.

Bumble Bee

Materials
30 × 23cm black felt
30 × 10cm yellow felt
20 × 35cm yellow fur fabric
20 × 35cm black fur fabric
10 × 10cm thin card
black and yellow embroidery cottons
1 black ball nose 20mm
1 pair of safety joggle eyes 20mm
60cm matching ribbon 12mm wide
matching thread
stuffing
scraps of yellow and white felt for flower

Method
1 Cut out the material making sure the arrows on the head and body sections lie the same way as the pile on the fur fabric. You require:
   2 body and 3 head sections in yellow fur
   4 body and 1 head section in black fur
   8 wing pieces in yellow felt
   2 brims, 1 top and 1 side of hat in black felt
   6 soles and 12 boot sides in black felt
   1 inner and 1 outer flower petal in felt
   1 inner hat brim in card
2 Mark on 1 yellow head section the positions for the nose and eyes. Mark on 2 yellow body sections the position for the wings.

Head
1 With right sides together join 3 yellow head pieces along the side seams CD, with the marked section in the middle.

2 Make tiny holes where the 3 marks are on the fur fabric and push through the shanks of the eyes and nose. Fasten these with the washers.
3 Stitch in the black head section (which forms the back of the head) along both sides, leaving an opening for the stuffing.
4 Turn the head right side out and stuff evenly. Close the opening with ladder stitch.

Hat
1 Place 2 felt hat brims together and stitch around middle.
2 Sandwich the card inner brim between the felt and stitch together around the outer edge.
3 Take the hat side piece and sew the short edges together.
4 Stitch the brim to the side of the hat making sure the side seam is inside, and stitch the hat top in position.
5 Place the inner flower petal on top of the outer flower petal and stitch to hat top.
6 Lightly stuff the hat and stitch to the top of the head at a slight angle.

Wings
1 Place 2 wing pieces together and join by working 2 rows of double running stitch in black embroidery cotton (see pattern). Make the other 3 wings in the same way.

Body
1 With right sides together stitch 3 black body pieces along the side seams AB to make the back half of the body.
2 Stitch the remaining 3 body pieces together in the same way with the black piece in the middle for the front half of the body.
3 Tack the wings to the front half of the body, placing them on the right side of the fur fabric with side seam matching the edge of the wing and the wing pointing downwards. Tack the top wings on first and

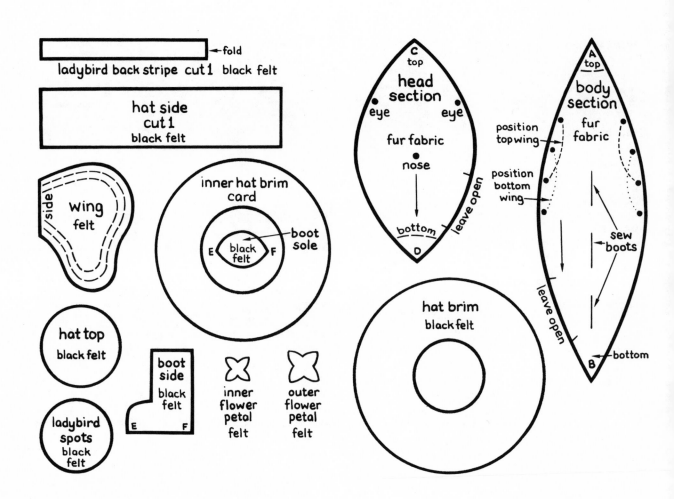

ladybird back stripe cut 1 black felt

hat side
cut 1
black felt

side

wing
felt

inner hat brim
card

boot
sole

E black
felt F

hat top

black felt

boot
side

black
felt

E   F

inner
flower
petal
felt

outer
flower
petal
felt

ladybird
spots
black
felt

fold

C
top

head
section

eye   eye

fur fabric

nose

bottom

leave open

D

A
top

body
section

position
top wing

fur
fabric

position
bottom
wing

sew
boots

leave open

bottom

B

hat brim
black felt

enlarge × 2

36

then the bottom wings overlapping the top wings.

4 With right sides together join the back and front body sections enclosing the wings and leaving a gap for stuffing.

5 Turn the body to the right side and stuff. Ladder stitch the opening.

6 Slipstitch the head to the top of the body.

Boots

1 Stitch 2 side boot seams together leaving the top and bottom open.

2 Stitch in the sole and then stuff the boot. Make 5 more the same.

3 Slipstitch the 6 boots on to the yellow sections of body front as marked on the pattern piece.

4 With yellow embroidery cotton, thread boot laces and tie in bows.

To complete, tie a length of ribbon around the neck.

Ladybird

Materials
30 x 30cm black felt
20 x 43cm black fur fabric
20 x 28cm red fur fabric
10 x 10cm thin card
red embroidery cotton
1 red ball nose 20mm
1 pair of safety joggle eyes 20mm
60cm matching ribbon 12mm wide
matching thread
stuffing
scraps of yellow and white felt for flower

Method

1 Cut out the material making sure that the arrows on the head and body sections lie the same way as the pile on the fur fabric. You require:
3 body and 3 head sections in black fur
3 body and 1 head section in red fur
2 brims, 1 top and 1 side of hat, 6 soles and 12 sides of boot, 8 wings, 1 black stripe and 4 spots all in black felt
1 inner and 1 outer flower petal in felt
1 inner hat brim in card

2 Mark positions for the wings on 2 black body sections. Mark position for the nose and eyes on 1 black head section.

3 Head. Make this the same as for the bee but use 3 black head pieces instead of yellow and use 1 red head piece instead of black.

4 Hat, wings and boots. As for bee.

5 Body. Follow the instructions for bee but use 3 red pieces for back half of the body and 3 black pieces for front half of the body.

6 When the back half of the body has been joined together, stitch on the right side of the fabric the black stripe down the centre piece and stitch 2 black felt dots either side of the stripe.

37

Lamb Stool

Mollie Mordle-Barnes, Horndean, Hants

This lifelike toy lamb is also a handy seat. He would be a welcome addition to any child's bedroom or playroom.

Materials

0.35m fluffy white fur fabric
30×30cm black felt
45×22×4cm deep foam
40×20cm 5-ply wood or chipboard
set of 23cm screw-on legs, black – or paint them yourself – with fixing plates and screws
stuffing for head
pair of teddy bear eyes
scrap of white felt or vinyl (for eyes)
scraps of coloured felt, including green
green ribbon or cord to go around neck
pink or red wool to mark nose and mouth

Method

1   Make pattern for head (no turnings allowed). Mark out 3cm squares on a piece of strong paper 35×27cm. Outline the various pieces as on plan, marking notches and numbers.

2   From fur fabric cut off a piece approximately 56×31cm with pile running lengthwise for body. Allowing 1cm turnings, cut out side head and back head gusset in fur fabric with pile as indicated. Cut two pieces for tail 8×27cm. In felt, cut face pieces, face gusset, two pairs of ears. Cut one pair white eye shapes.

3   Shape corners of board by measuring off 4cm along edges at each corner and marking across diagonally. Saw off corners and rub down with sandpaper.

4   Arrange metal plates on board as shown. Make sure higher edge of shaped circle faces away from board edge. Screw plates down.

5   Place board on table with metal plates underneath. Arrange foam piece over it. Trim off surplus, leaving 2cm overlapping all round. Now place fur fabric body piece over foam, pinning here and there to hold. At one end, turn edge of fur fabric under, level with lower edge of board. Put in two or three 2cm-long panel pins to hold. Stretch fur fabric firmly and insert panel pins into turned-in edges at opposite end. Now turn in edges of each side and nail down in same manner. Leave corners until last. Here, form a pleat at each corner and cut off surplus. Turn in edges carefully keeping fabric taut and tack down.

6   Pin and tack side head pieces to back head gusset from (A) to (B). Join front neck seam (C) to (D) matching all notches. Join face pieces to front head gusset from (E) to (F) matching notches. Stitch seams. Set face to head with top of back and front head gussets matching and seams coinciding. Pin and tack remaining edges together. Stitch. Turn head to right side and stuff very firmly. Place ear pieces together in pairs, tack, stitch and turn to right side. Turn under and oversew bottom edges.

7   Place tail pieces together, fur side inside, pin, tack and stitch entire length rounding off at tail end. Turn to right side.

8   Place head on body with pile on body flowing away from head, and front of neck set back 3cm from front edge. Starting at front neck, using strong thread and long needle, oversew neck to body, turning edges under as you proceed, pulling head down firmly. Go round several times. Fasten off strongly.

9   Place ears on head at join of fur cloth and felt, allowing 8cm space between. Stitch firmly to head, forming a natural curve at bottom.

10   Cut wire between eyes, and with small pliers form a loop. Cut off surplus wire and bend ends in. Cut a slit in centre of each white eye piece and pass loop through. With darning needle and strong thread, place eye in correct position. Stitch through face to opposite eye position, and attach to other eye. Take thread inside from eye to eye several times. Fasten off securely. If felt eyes are preferred cut two 1cm circles from black felt and glue on to centre of each

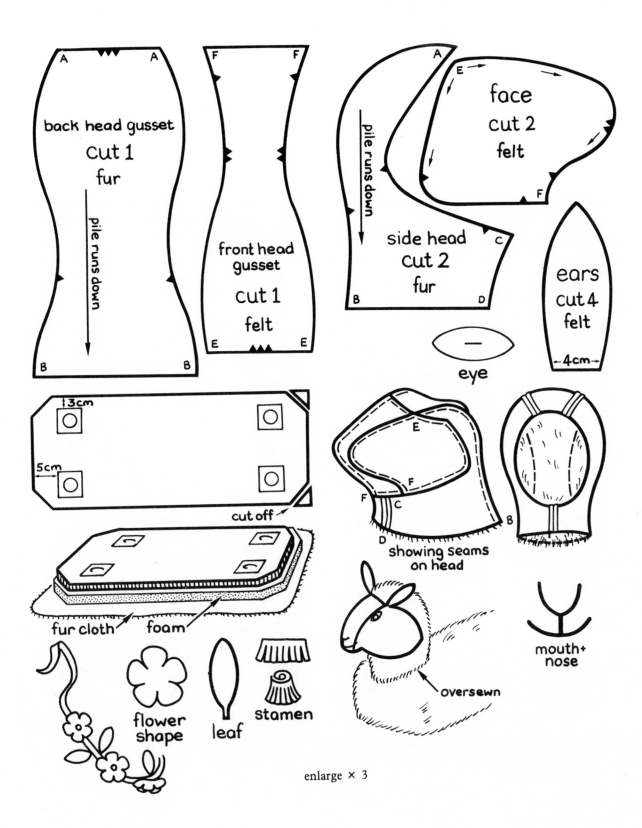

back head gusset
cut 1
fur

pile runs down

A A
B B

front head gusset
cut 1
felt

F F
E E

pile runs down

side head
cut 2
fur

A
B
C
D

face
cut 2
felt

E
F

ears
cut 4
felt

4cm

eye

3cm

5cm

cut off

fur cloth   foam

showing seams
on head

E
F
C
B
D

overswen

mouth+
nose

flower
shape

leaf

stamen

enlarge × 3

white eye piece. Place eyes on head and glue or stitch invisibly into position.

11 With pink or red wool, work outline of nose and mouth as illustration shows.

12 Lay tail along centre of body with curved end towards head, straight end close to opposite end of body. Oversew very strongly and fold tail down.

13 To make necklace (optional), cut out petal shapes in coloured felt as shown. Cut leaves in green. Arrange and stitch to green ribbon or cord. Place around lamb's neck and tie. Finally, release all trapped pile along seams with a bodkin or fine steel knitting needle. Brush up pile on head and body. Screw on legs.

Rabbit

Jo Watson, Ilkley, West Yorks

This one basic pattern can be easily adapted to make a cat or dog as well by changing the ears, nose and tail. Made of fur fabric, it is extremely cuddly.

Materials
0.25m fur fabric
animal safety eyes
scraps of felt
ribbon
stuffing

Method

1 Cut 25cm diameter circle for body, 18cm diameter circle for head. On the smaller circle mark the position of the eyes – 12mm from the centre and 5cm apart. Cut out 4 ear shapes and a 9.5cm circle for tail.

2 With strong thread run a gathering thread 10mm inside the edge of both head and body circles and gently gather together.

3 Stuff body firmly until you have a round ball shape. If using animal safety eyes, insert the eyes in the head then stuff as for body.

4 With strong thread sew the two parts firmly together.

5 With right sides facing sew ears together, turn, and sew in position on head.

6 Gather round edge of tail circle, stuff and sew into position.

7 Cut nose shape in felt and sew in position, adding mouth and whiskers in wool. Tie a length of ribbon around neck. If felt eyes are preferred, sew pupil to main eye and then sew into position on head.

enlarge × 1½

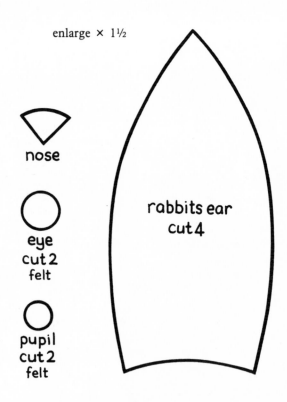

nose

eye
cut 2
felt

pupil
cut 2
felt

rabbits ear
cut 4

Nursery Book
Shirley A. Mundy, Southsea

A book with a difference for this one is made out of fabric with illustrations worked in appliqué. It is soft, washable, not easily damaged and can be individually made to suit the toddler. It measures 21×22.5cm.

Materials
0.5m calico or washable fabric
50g terylene wadding
iron-on interfacing
sewing thread
scraps of different-textured washable fabric

enlarge × 1¾

Method

1 From calico cut 4 pieces 46×25cm.
2 Make separate pattern for each appliqué shape and one for two centre pages of book. The dotted lines on the diagram indicate where one piece of fabric overlaps another.
3 Iron interfacing on to back of fabric scraps, then use your patterns to cut out appliqué shapes from stiffened fabric. The interfacing helps to stop fabric from fraying and puckering when sewing.
4 Arrange appliqué shapes on to one piece of fabric, placing and overlapping the pieces where necessary. Tack shapes into place. Set your machine to a close stitch length, maximum stitch width and zigzag sew all round pieces except where dotted lines are shown on diagram.
5 Mark centres on three remaining pieces of fabric. Using designs on centre pages, choose two shapes for each piece of fabric and work them in appliqué. (Thus you might combine the sun and the swing.) Sew as before.
6 To add extra texture and interest embroider details on pictures.
7 To complete book place 2 right-side pieces together, then a piece of wadding. Tack into place. Machine round edge leaving·an opening to turn it through to right side. Repeat with other 2 pieces. Slip stitch opening.
8 Press all sides. Place pages together, find centre and tack in place. Sew 2 rows of stitching for strength.

Penguin
Linda Crowther, Thornbury, Avon

A charming, really cuddly creature. By using brown, gold and white fur fabric for the body and brown and orange felt for features etc, he can become an owl.

Materials

30×35cm black fur fabric
30×25cm white fur fabric
12×12cm orange felt
5×10cm white felt
4×8cm blue felt
pair 16mm blue safety eyes
stuffing

Method

1 Cut out pieces; 5mm seam allowance throughout.
2 Right sides together, sew 1 black wing to corresponding white wing leaving straight edges open. Sew other pair in the same way. Turn right sides out.
3 Matching points A and B, right sides together, sew centre front to side fronts (a). Note that these seams will be curved.
4 Fold beak in half, corner to corner and baste to one headpiece on right side. Right sides together sew head to front body (b).
5 Right sides together sew back head to back body leaving an opening for turning.
6 Right sides together sew two parts of body together down side seams, incorporating wings – black part of wing to black part of body (c). Leave bottom open.
7 Insert base, matching points C, and sew to body.
8 Turn penguin right side out.
9 Assemble eyes and felt pieces as shown (d), making small holes in felt for stem.
10 Attach eyes to head using orange felt offcuts inside.
11 Stuff firmly and ladder stitch opening.
12 Release any fur trapped in seams using a bodkin, and brush penguin to finish.

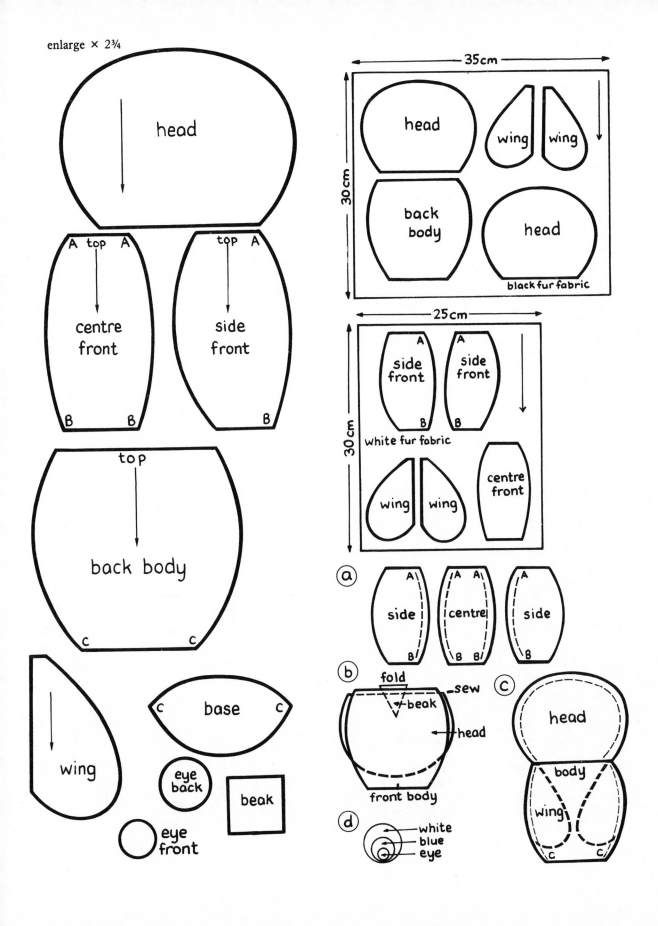

enlarge × 2¾

head

A top A
top A

centre
front

side
front

B B
B

top

back body

C C

wing

base
C C

eye
back

beak

eye
front

35cm

head

wing wing

back
body

head

black fur fabric

30cm

25cm

side
front
A

side
front
A

B B

white fur fabric

wing wing

centre
front

30cm

(a) side A | A | A centre A | side
B B | B B

(b) fold
sew
beak
head
front body

(c) head
body
wing
C C

(d) white
blue
eye

Buzz Bee

Linda Crowther, Thornbury, Avon

A cheerful bee to buzz up and down in a child's bedroom on elastic.

Materials
45 × 30cm black fur fabric
25 × 30cm gold fur fabric
12 × 12cm white fur fabric
6 × 6cm white felt
pair 16mm blue safety eyes
stuffing
50cm round elastic or cord
ribbon

Method
1 Cut out the patterns as illustrated; 5mm seams are used throughout. Cut 2 circles the size of a 5p piece from white felt. Save offcuts to use when inserting eyes.
2 Right sides together, sew 1 black wing to 1 gold wing leaving straight edge open. Turn right side out. Repeat with other pair.
3 Right sides of tail together, bring points B together and sew from A to B.
4 Right sides together, sew stripes in order shown (a). Cut last black stripe along dotted lines of pattern.
5 Right sides together, match points H, F, E and D and sew from D to E (b).
6 Place wings with black sides together and insert inside body matching points E and F. Sew through all layers as shown, from E to H.
7 Right sides together, insert tail in tapered end of body, matching D on body with G on tail. Sew tail to body from G through B to G again.
8 Run a gathering thread around edge of head circle and draw up to fit open end of body. Right sides together, insert head in open end of body, matching point C on head with points H on body. Sew head to

body leaving an opening for turning opposite point C and distributing gathers evenly. Turn right side out.
9 Cut a small hole in centre of each white felt circle and push stem of eye through. Insert eyes in head, wide apart and slightly above centre.
10 Tie a large knot in one end of elastic or cord and, using a bodkin, thread through body seam at F, with knot inside body.
11 Stuff bee firmly, rounding out and shaping head – the 'face' should be fairly flat. Ladder stitch opening.
12 Release any fur trapped in seams using a bodkin, and brush bumble bee. Make a loop in free end of elastic or cord and finish with ribbon bow.

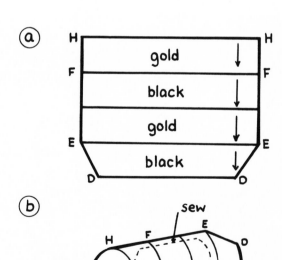

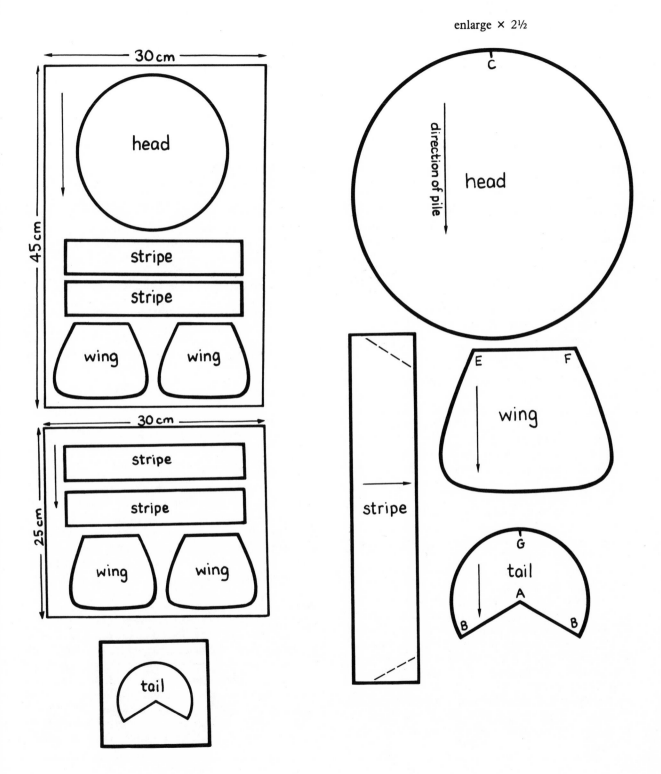

enlarge × 2½

30 cm

45 cm

head

stripe

stripe

wing   wing

30 cm

25 cm

stripe

stripe

wing   wing

tail

direction of pile

head

C

stripe

E   F

wing

G

tail

A

B   B

WALL HANGINGS *illustrated in colour on page 28*

Jute Hanging
Eileen Thompson, Crawley, Sussex

This is an interesting hanging to enhance a plain wall, yet it is simply a matter of knotting jute. It measures 30×75cm but the size can be adjusted to fit your requirements.

Materials
73m medium jute
6mm dowel 32cm long
2 large wooden beads to fix on end of dowel
oddments of various texture and colour yarn
assorted wooden beads

Method
1   Cut 20 3.6m lengths of jute. Fold each in half and fix to dowel with lark's head knots. Using alternating square knots to work background, work approximately 50cm length. Finish with overhand knots in pairs of cords to make fringe.
2   Either work out a design on paper or use wool or yarn at random to create a design on the jute background. If you do not like the result it is quite easy to take the yarn off and start again.
3   If you only have ordinary yarn available you can make your own textures by crocheting lengths of wool in single chain with picots here and there, or by knitting and plaiting before use.
4   Weave your yarn in and out of the background, leaving loops at random for effect. To finish just leave ends hanging. Long and short lengths of wool can be knotted into the background using a crochet hook to make tassels. This design has wooden beads from an old necklace sewn on to the background. There is no need to be fussy about your stitches!
5   The fringe is finished off by frapping (binding tightly) ends of jute here and there.
6   The dowel is finished off with a large-holed bead at either end. Knot a length of jute to dowel for hanging. Dab ends of knots with clear-drying glue to secure.

Dried Flower Picture
Yvonne Smalley, Weston-on-Trent, Derbyshire

The colours and textures of the materials used in this collage look very rich, yet many of these materials can be collected on a Sunday afternoon walk in the country.

Materials
offcut of hardboard (size to suit your own requirement)
screw-in hook
frame to fit the hardboard (either second-hand from jumble sale, do-it-yourself kit or ready-made)
offcut velvet or hessian in plain colour, ie dark brown or black velvet, natural or dyed hessian (slightly larger than headboard)
Copydex glue
4 small panel pins (to nail completed picture into frame)
stiff card for backing
piece of bark (taken *only* from a dead tree)
fir cones, nuts and cases, dried seed pods, dried grasses, everlasting flowers (especially helichrysums), dyed grasses, etc

Home-made flowers
You cannot always find a suitable flower for your picture so have a try at making your own. Take a large cone with soft 'petals' and cut off five or six of these 'petals'. Put a dab of Copydex on the end of each piece, leave for a few seconds then assemble in the shape of a flower. Finally glue a small, everlasting flower in the centre, with tiny flowers around this (a).

Method
1   Put the piece of velvet wrong-side-up on a table and place the piece of hardboard on top (if using hessian, the material must first be pressed under a damp cloth using a hot iron). Put glue all round the edges of the hardboard then, working on one side at a time, fold the edge of the velvet on to the hardboard stretching the velvet slightly to achieve a smooth, wrinkle-free finish (b). Continue in this way until all four sides are completed. To neaten the corners, cut a triangle off

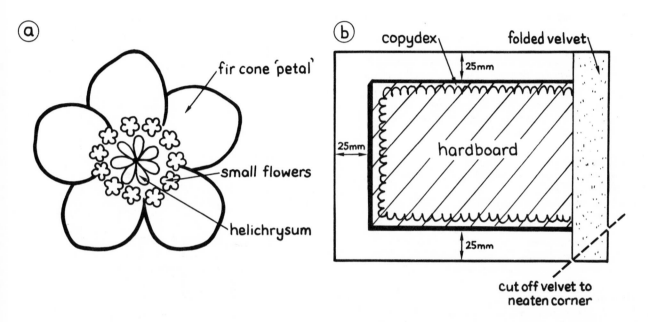

(a) fir cone 'petal'

small flowers

helichrysum

(b) copydex   folded velvet

25mm

25mm

hardboard

25mm

cut off velvet to
neaten corner

each and fold the remaining velvet on to the hardboard.

2　Take the piece of bark and, either freehand or using a
paper pattern, cut out the shape of a vase using a
sharp knife. Alternatively, you can use some stiff
stalks and make the flower picture into a bouquet.
Put the bark vase on the velvet leaving a suitable
margin below and an equal margin each side of the
vase. Do not glue yet – it is much better to experi-
ment with your design until you are perfectly
satisfied with the result.

3　Beginning in the centre, place your selected flowers
and cones, using the larger ones first and grading
them until you reach the edge of the design, here
using your smallest flowers, nuts and cones. When
you are satisfied with the effect, glue on the vase and
then start to glue on the various pieces, again starting
from the centre. Be careful to put each item close to

the next; you may have to fill-in with extra small
flowers at the edge of the design. Sometimes the
helichrysums close when they have been glued but
do not panic – they usually open up again when the
glue has dried (this will take a few hours). White
spirit will remove any spilt Copydex. When the glue
is completely dry turn your picture upside down to
check that all the items have been firmly glued.

4　Now frame the picture (if the background colour is
dark use a light-coloured frame or vice versa). Nail
one panel pin on each side of the frame on the wrong
side and fix a small hook at the top back centre of the
frame. Glue a piece of card on to the back of the
picture to within 5mm of the edge of the frame.
Finally, apply a thin coat of clear varnish to your
bark vase to give it a gloss finish and seal it against
damp.

Shell Calendar

Barbara W. Frame, East Kilbride

A calendar, simply and delicately made using natural materials which can be collected on a seaside walk. It is surprising just how many different kinds of shells there are; even broken shells with attractive curves worn smooth by the tides look well if suitably placed. Pebbles, too, are good for the centres of shell flowers.

Materials
card of required size (deckle-edged card can be used)
19cm ribbon 12mm wide
11cm gold or silver passepartout
1 calendar tab
glue
a few everlasting leaves
shells and small pebbles
cellophane paper to cover picture (optional)

Method
1   Cut ribbon to give two 5cm and one 9cm lengths.
2   Turn card and tab face down and glue all three pieces of ribbon to the card and tab.
3   Cut passepartout into three 4cm lengths. Cut off all the corners and stick each piece in turn over the ragged ends of ribbon with a little glue (a). Allow to dry.
4   On a piece of paper the same shape as the card, arrange your shells to form a pleasing design. When you are satisfied with the result, pick up each shell or leaf one by one and place it on the calendar in an identical position.
5   A butterfly design is effective and simple to make. Just add two shells that are joined together, laid out open and flat. Add two small pieces of thick thread as feelers and you have a tiny butterfly.
6   Cover with cellophane and add small label to back, if you wish, stating where the shells came from.

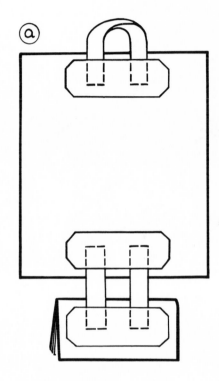

Three-Dimensional Découpage

Mary Avery, London N10

The delightful art of découpage started in the seventeenth century in Venice when the Venetian cabinetmakers were seeking a less expensive way of decorating their furniture. The word is French for 'to cut paper' and basically paper prints were cut out, coloured and then stuck on to the furniture. The surface was then covered with many layers of varnish which was rubbed down between coats, and further coats applied, until the surface was completely smooth.

This art can still be practised today to decorate wood, glass, metal, lampshades, etc, and many types of picture are readily available such as greetings cards, wrapping paper, or more sophisticated prints.

Three-dimensional découpage differs in that a picture is

48

'built up' using 4, 5 or even 6 layers of thin paper.
Wrapping paper is the most suitable as a sheet usually gives
this number of copies of the same design.

Materials

tube of translucent silicone rubber sealant (Dow Corning or
  Evo-Stik, obtainable from good hardware or DIY shops)
small sharp scissors
cocktail stick
tissues
working base (piece of corrugated card, ceiling tile, cork tile, etc)
pins
small tweezers (optional)
spray varnish (optional)

Method

1 Choose a simple design such as a figure, and cut out
  two copies. If the person is standing on grass, or has
  shadow round its feet this can remain on the base
  copy. Using two or three plain dressmaking pins,
  lightly attach the base copy to your working base.
  You are now ready to start the 'building up' process.

2 Use the rubber sealant straight from the tube and
  squeeze gently from the bottom. With a cocktail stick
  take off a globule about the size of a small pea, and
  place it on the centre of the head. Working down the
  figure place further globules at 'contact points'. The
  number will obviously vary according to the size of
  the figure, but usually 5 or 6 will be sufficient, the
  idea being to raise the second copy evenly above the
  base copy. Place the second copy lightly on the
  globules, taking care not to press them down, and
  leave to set (10–15min). Clean cocktail stick with
  tissue before sealant sets.

3 While your work is setting start cutting out further
  copies of your picture, and assess which parts of the
  picture you are going to use for each successive layer.
  Basically in the third picture cut away any parts that
  you want to recede into the background, ie legs and
  face, side panels of skirt, etc, and adhere remaining
  parts of picture as before.

4 With the fourth picture cut out dress, hair – which
  you may find you can snip finely to give a more
  realistic effect, hat, etc. To give these parts more
  'movement' you will find that by holding the paper in
  one hand and slowly running it between the thumb
  of the other hand and the side edge of your scissors
  you will get a curve. You will probably now find it
  easier to apply the adhesive to these parts and the
  globules will vary in size as the pieces get smaller.
  Tweezers are also useful in placing these parts.

5 Your work will now be taking on surprising
  dimension and you will easily be able to see if you
  wish to raise further sections with parts from your
  remaining pictures. These will probably be an
  apron, hat, bows, shoes, flowers, etc, and you will
  now find your figure looking most realistic.

6 The finished picture can be given a coat of spray
  varnish while it is still on the working base, and
  allowed to dry before mounting.

7 Mounts can be very varied. They can be plain-
  coloured card, or card covered with wallpaper, velvet
  fablon, material, hessian, etc. Other backgrounds can
  be cork, a small plain tile, or mounted in a normal
  picture frame. Adhesive hangers for your mounts can
  be obtained from art shops, or stationers selling art
  materials.

8 Having completed a figure, the possibilities for
  further pictures are endless, depending on wrapping
  paper with suitable potential. Use fairly bold
  pictures that are not too difficult to cut out; sprays of
  flowers can be most effective, especially if you curve
  prominent leaves and petals before sticking in place.

Poster Collage
Maureen E. Murphy, Chester

You do not need any design or drawing skills to make this delightful collage. The design is based on a poster – so that all you have to do is to interpret the outline of the original design in your own way.

Materials
2 copies of poster, birthday card or similar
glue
thin card for backing (same size as frame)
calico for backing picture
oddments of material
trimmings: lace, beads, ribbon
cotton wool for padding
needle and cotton
felt tips or embroidery silks for facial features
frame (optional)

Method
1 Select your illustration. It is easiest to use the same size as the illustration but an enlargement can easily be made using graph paper.
2 The simplest method is to buy two identical posters and to cut one out like a jigsaw, keeping each item (eg hat) whole. Keep each shape in place so that you can see how the pieces fit together.
3 Cut the wool into small pieces and glue to the hair shape making sure none of the picture is showing through.
4 Cut pink felt for face and arms, and glue to face and arms shapes.
5 Continue covering all the shapes with oddments of material until you have finished.
6 If you want an article of clothing to stand out, eg the rag doll's apron, then gather it slightly with needle and cotton before glueing it to the shape.
7 The little girl's bonnet and dress are padded out to give a fuller shape. This is simply done by glueing cotton wool on before covering with material.

8 When you have finished covering all the shapes and have added the trimmings, allow the shapes to dry.
9 Meanwhile prepare the backing by covering card of the required shape with calico or background material. Glue the edges of the backing material to the back of the card. In this way the glue will not show through and spoil your picture.
10 Once the backing is dry you are ready to assemble your picture. Using the uncut poster as a guide, place the jigsaw pieces together on to the calico and assemble into a picture.

Wild Oat Marquetry
Berniece M. Hansard, Lincoln

This picture is based on John Constable's 'Cottage in a Cornfield', leaving out the donkey and adding a full moon as the picture is mounted on black velvet. You may wish to use a similar picture or make your own design. Simple things are often the most effective. Windmills are good; wagons and carts look good in the rich colours of straw. Wheels are difficult to do but made easier if you find a piece of straw with a natural curve in it. Always mount the parts separately, eg the mill body, then the sails; or the wagon body adding the shafts and wheels later. 22×27cm.

Materials
prepared oats
22×27cm black velvet
25×20cm thick card or cardboard
greaseproof paper
glue pen such as UHU or Bostik
tweezers

50

Preparation of Oats

Gather the oats and hang up to dry. The best colours – which range from browns to deepest gold and palest silver – are to be found in ripe oats but gather some unripe ones too, for they provide a variety of green shades. The whole of the plant can be used and they can be dyed – boil them in a double strength dye and lay on old sacks to dry. When ready to make your picture, prepare your straw by first soaking it for several minutes in cold water, then wrap it in an old towel and leave for an hour or so to temper. Sort the leaves from the stalks and iron them with a hot iron on brown paper. This is your picture material.

Method

1 Cut velvet to fit card, glue extreme edges to card, taking care to leave no wrinkles and to use glue sparingly.
2 Draw or trace picture to finished size. Use this as your guide for the placing of the cottage, fence, gate, tree and moon.
3 Trace cottage on to greaseproof paper.
4 Cut out windows, cut and stick slivers of straw and make a lattice work for the windows.
5 Using the various colours of straw, build up the cottage. When complete cut surplus greaseproof away. Set aside.
6 Trace five-barred gate on to greaseproof paper. Glue posts and top and bottom rails, cut paper away from middle and mount the other rails from the back. Set aside.
7 Glue strips of oat leaf straight on to the velvet backing. Mount cottage, small fence, five-barred gate and fencing, remembering to place horizontal posts down first so that the upright posts of fence are on top.
8 Mount tree freehand using the oat leaf for the trunk and the seed head for the top. Add a few seed heads round cottage and in foreground.
9 Mount the moon.

To Frame Your Picture

A ready-made frame can be used, but you may wish to make a straw frame.

Materials

clear acetate (obtainable from art dealers)
glue
Sellotape
25 × 20cm card
string to hang picture
brown paper
long strips of prepared oat stem

Method

1 Make two holes in cardboard and thread the string through for hanging but do not secure.
2 Cover picture with the acetate sheeting, having cut it sufficiently large enough to go to the back where it should be fastened down with Sellotape. Make very sure before fastening down that there are no loose straws or dust to mark it.
3 Glue the cardboard on to the back of the picture.
4 Take a piece of brown paper 2.5cm larger all round than the finished picture and make two holes to bring string through. Turn in 6mm all round. Glue down.
5 Place picture face upwards on to paper, bring the 6mm double fold of paper on to acetate sheet, neaten corners, glue down.
6 Cut straw strips to size, glue on to brown paper border to make the frame.

Choco the Clown
Margaret Edwards, Codsall, Wolverhampton

Choco, who is illustrated in colour on page 61, was designed to show the larger-than-life features of a clown, and to make him a fun character. He was mostly worked in zig-zag stitch using a swing-needle machine.

Materials
1.2m of 95cm wide brushed denim or similar weight fabric for backing and lining. Flesh colour was obtained by dyeing white calico in a mixture of strong coffee and red ink
small pieces of felt in lime green, white, black, red and yellow
orange rug wool or thick knitting wool for hair
scraps of appropriate fabrics for vest, trousers, socks, cuffs and braces (thin leather or plastic leather cloth is ideal for these)
2 small gilt trouser buttons
6 eyelets for shoes
leather strips for soles
3 table-tennis balls
assorted linings for covering balloons
embroidery thread for strings
length of bamboo cane and cord for hanging
large piece of white paper big enough for finished master drawing of clown 52.5 × 37.5cm plus tracing pattern paper of the same size for tracing design

Method

Design
1   Enlarge drawing of Choco as follows: taking each square at a time, transfer the lines that are in the squares to a large sheet of paper ruled into 2.5cm squares, thus enlarging the design as you progress. Rule in outside edge of frame.
2   This scaled-up clown is now your master drawing and is kept intact, perhaps to be used again. All subsequent information is traced off. Ink in the design and outside frame with a fine-tipped pen so that the design is easier to see when tracing through.
3   Place tracing paper over drawing and carefully trace

finished wall hanging 52·5cm × 37·5cm

through, including frame edge, Sellotaping the two layers together to stop any movement while you work. Cut round frame edge of tracing.
4   The tracing is now complete and you have the pattern required to transfer design to fabric.

Cutting out and preparation
1   Pin pattern to lining fabric on straight of grain and cut round; no turnings are required.

52

2 Place pattern on backing fabric and pin round, using small firm tacking stitches to outline frame edge. (This is important because this line is a stitching and turning line to be used when finishing off wallhanging.) Before cutting out, allow 3cm on side seams and bottom, and 8cm for top. If your backing fabric is inclined to fray, leave more seam allowance and cut to size when collage is completed.

3 The collage is made up of layers, the first layer being the face and chest. This section is stitched on first and, so that a lot of ugly edges are not visible, these pattern pieces are made larger where they underlap the next layer. These lines are shown as dotted lines and are called placement lines; they can be stitched on to give the position of parts and those threads which do not show can be left in place.

4 Mark in other lines such as around the head, the balloon strings, and between shoe and sole and trouser position. The face features can be applied without marking the face first and the bow tie is added afterwards. The braces are secured at the shoulder and a buttonhole is cut to fit the trouser buttons.

5 When you are satisfied that all important lines have been marked, remove the pattern.

Making up
Use master drawing for all pattern pieces and extend to placement lines where shown.

1 Start with face and chest, arms and hands, and socks.

2 When cutting out trousers and cuffs notice that they are giving the appearance of going round the back of the body. On your pattern pieces cut out the 'back' section right across and then cut back, leaving enough fabric to turn under on fitting lines. Emphasise this feature by making an inner row of machining.

3 Face. This is worked in felt – each section worked by hand using a hemming stitch.

4 To work the nose, cut a circle 2.5cm and run a gathering thread around the edge. Pack a small quantity of filling inside, pull up to make a ball shape and sew in place.

5 Attach the eyelets to the shoes, and cut yellow felt in strips for laces. Secure laces at back of work to stop ends coming out of holes. Toes of shoes are padded, so after hemming shoe all round as far as toe-cap line, stitch across toe-cap line. Pack toe with kapok and hem round.

6 The hair is twisted round to form circles and couched in place.

7 The bent fingers are back-stitched by hand.

8 Work balloon strings in stem stitch going 'under' fingers as shown. Balloons are applied after lining is put on.

9 Lining. Working from the back with wrong sides together pin lining to backing fabric on frame line. Tack round. Turn to right side and machine bottom and sides just inside of the frame line catching lining to backing fabric. Make a 2cm hem on sides and bottom of wallhanging mitring the corners. Hem round. Take out tacking threads and press hem from right side. Make a heading channel for bamboo cane by turning under 2cm and placing edge just below top frame line concealing lining edge. Turn work to right side and machine just inside frame line to line up with side frame lines. This outer frame line looks effective worked in a zig-zag stitch.

10 Balloons. Cut table-tennis balls in half and smooth edges. Make a 10cm circle pattern for covering balloons. Using double thread and working 7cm from the edge run a gathering line round outer edge. Put half ball inside and pull up making fabric as taut as you can. Fasten off securely and take thread to outer edge. Place balloon in position and hem round.

11 The bow tie is just a straight strip of fabric folded back into the centre, it is secured by the 'knot' which is a small strip of fabric taken and hemmed in place.

12 Slide through the bamboo cane and make a loop in each end of the cord.

Little Girl Collage

Margaret Edwards, Codsall, Wolverhampton

An endearing little study which can be worked quickly with oddments of wool, felt and fabric, either with a zig-zag machine stitch or by hand if non-fraying materials are used. The large hat and roomy cape make difficult hands and face unnecessary.

Materials

16.4 × 21.4cm picture frame (8 × 6in standard frame size)
15.4 × 20.4cm frame window – firm perspex or acetate would be safer and thinner than glass
15.4 × 20.4cm firm fabric for mounting collage eg calico, denim
oddments of fabric for outfit
narrow ribbon for hair
wool for plait
leather or felt for shoes
glue
embroidery thread for basket
felt, small buttons and beads for trimming

Method

1 Using diagram, trace off complete collage and cut round outer edge of frame. Using this as your pattern, cut out mounting fabric.
2 Cut out little girl and basket keeping them in one piece. Position on mounting fabric and pin round.
3 Mark guidelines on mounting fabric to enable you to position each section of collage, but the marks must not be visible on finished work. If the edges are to be zig-zagged, a fine pencil line can be used. If embroidery is to be used then mark lines with thread.
4 Trace individual pattern pieces off the diagram.
5 Make up the collage as if dressing the little girl, from the skin outwards. Where one layer underlaps a top layer, an allowance is made on the pattern piece so that it can be tucked underneath to give a neat appearance and the top layer is stitched across all layers, eg hair and cape are extended to fit under hat, and dress and pinny extend under cape. Each pattern piece in turn is secured in place slightly away from the edge to avoid machine stitch.
6 Legs are worked in back stitch, sides and bottom of basket in stem stitch, handle of basket in open chain stitch and top of basket in Pekinese stitch. The body of the basket is lattice stitch – loose thread forming a square and held in place at intersections.

NB Keep collage to minimum thickness so that your finished work will fit comfortably in the frame.

finished size 20·4 cm x 15·4 cm

PUPPETS *illustrated in colour on page 61*

Nursery Rhyme Finger Puppets
Vera A. Parsons, High Wycombe, Bucks

These felt finger puppets, 7.5cm high, are great fun when used to illustrate or retell a story. They are easy to make and in no time you can compile a story book of characters.

Humpty Dumpty and Soldiers

Materials
10×5cm red felt
14×5cm flesh-coloured felt
15×12.5cm black felt
10×7.5cm blue or turquoise felt
scraps of gold and white felt
Copydex adhesive
fabric paints or felt marker pens in black, red and white.

Method
Cut out the following pieces, same size as pattern:

Soldiers	*Humpty Dumpty*
2 bodies in red	1 body blue or turquoise
2 faces in flesh	1 face in flesh
2 hats in black	2 collars in white
2 plumes in gold	1 bowtie in gold
2 collars in black	
2 front bands in black	

Soldiers
1 Glue face to body where they overlap.
2 Glue hat to face where they overlap.
3 Glue on collar, front band and plume – leave to dry.
4 On the *wrong* side, put a strip of glue all around outside edge except base using a fine brush. Place on backing, holding down firmly for 10 seconds.
5 When firmly stuck and glue is dry, cut around edges, carefully trimming off any overlaps on collar and front band.
6 Add nose and mouth in red fabric paint; use a fine brush for mouth, while the end of a piece of dowelling dipped in paint and printed down makes a nice round nose. Alternatively use felt-tip pens.

Humpty Dumpty
1 Glue face to body as for Soldier.
2 Glue collar to overlap where face and body join.
3 Glue on bowtie at centre. Leave to dry.
4 Glue all round on *wrong* side leaving bottom open and stick on to body-coloured felt.
5 When dry trim as for Soldier.
6 Paint hair on with black fabric paint. Use larger dowelling dipped in white for whites of eyes and when this has dried use smaller dowling and black paint for pupils. Nose is red as for Soldiers.

Goldilocks and the Three Bears

Materials
7.5×10cm green felt
4×4cm flesh coloured felt
6×7.5cm gold felt
18×15cm brown felt
scraps of white felt
Copydex adhesive
fabric paints or felt pens in blue, black and red

Method
Cut out the following pieces, same size as pattern:

Goldilocks	*Bears*
green body	3 brown bodies
flesh face	3 brown heads
gold hair	3 gold noses
white collar	6 white eyes

Make up as for Humpty Dumpty and Soldiers.

55

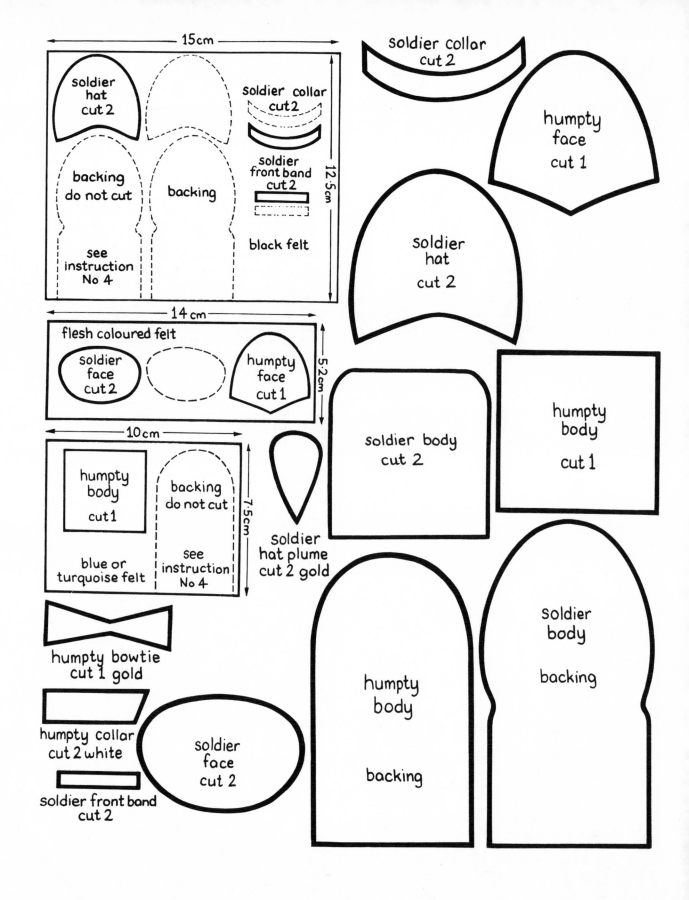

15cm

soldier
hat
cut 2

backing
do not cut

backing

see
instruction
No 4

12.5cm

soldier collar
cut 2

soldier
front band
cut 2

black felt

14 cm

flesh coloured felt

soldier
face
cut 2

humpty
face
cut 1

5.2cm

10cm

humpty
body
cut 1

backing
do not cut

7.5cm

blue or
turquoise felt

see
instruction
No 4

humpty bowtie
cut 1 gold

humpty collar
cut 2 white

soldier front band
cut 2

soldier collar
cut 2

humpty
face
cut 1

soldier
hat
cut 2

soldier body
cut 2

humpty
body
cut 1

soldier
hat plume
cut 2 gold

soldier
face
cut 2

humpty
body

backing

soldier
body

backing

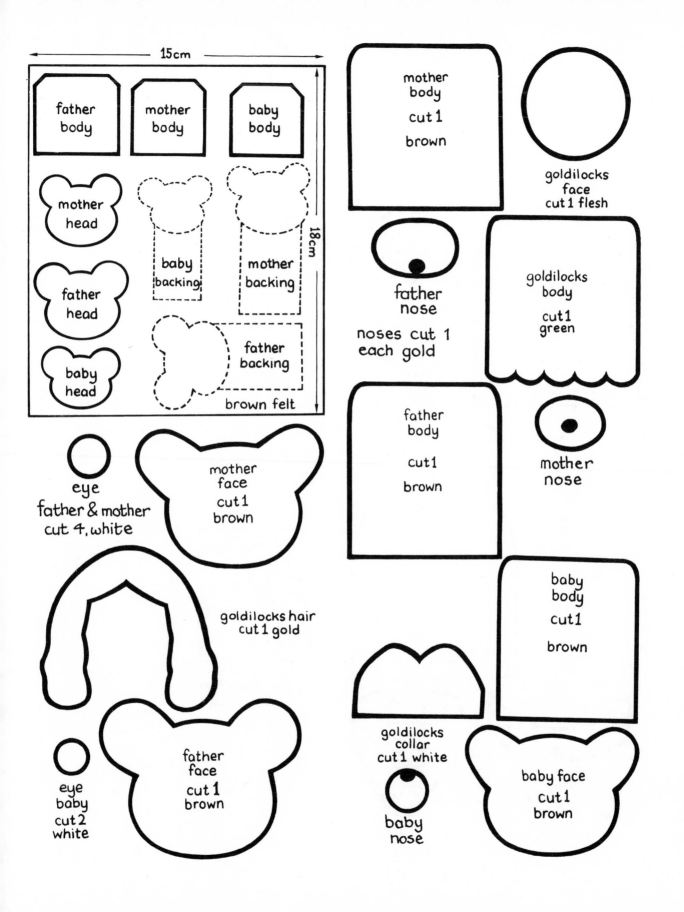

15cm

18cm

father body

mother body

baby body

mother head

baby backing

mother backing

father head

father backing

baby head

brown felt

mother body
cut 1
brown

goldilocks face
cut 1 flesh

father nose

noses cut 1 each gold

goldilocks body
cut 1 green

father body
cut 1 brown

mother nose

eye
father & mother
cut 4, white

mother face
cut 1 brown

goldilocks hair
cut 1 gold

baby body
cut 1 brown

eye baby
cut 2 white

father face
cut 1 brown

goldilocks collar
cut 1 white

baby nose

baby face
cut 1 brown

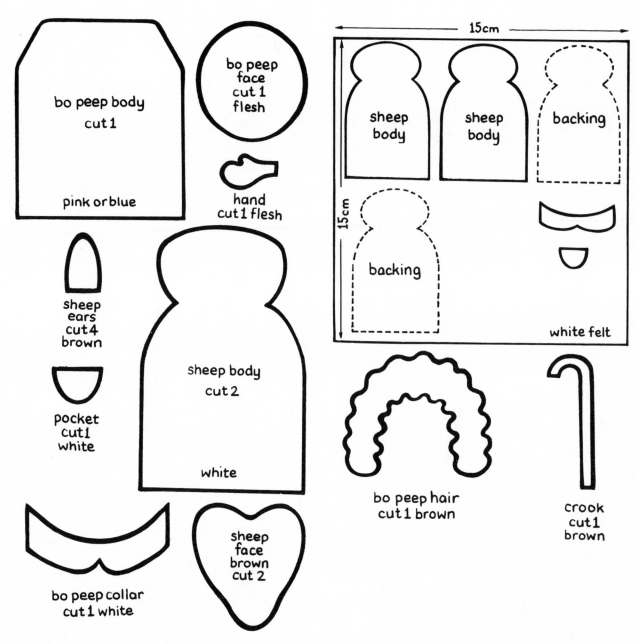

bo peep body
cut 1

pink or blue

bo peep
face
cut 1
flesh

hand
cut 1 flesh

15cm

sheep
body

sheep
body

backing

15cm

backing

white felt

sheep
ears
cut 4
brown

pocket
cut 1
white

sheep body
cut 2

white

bo peep hair
cut 1 brown

crook
cut 1
brown

bo peep collar
cut 1 white

sheep
face
brown
cut 2

Little Bo Peep and Sheep

Materials
7.5 × 10cm pink or blue felt
5 × 4cm flesh-coloured felt
15 × 15cm white felt
7.5 × 15cm brown felt
Copydex adhesive
fabric paint or felt-tip pens in blue, red and black

Method
Cut out the following pieces, same size as pattern:

Sheep	Bo Peep
2 bodies in white	1 body in pink or blue
2 heads in white	hair in brown
2 faces in brown	face in flesh
4 ears in brown	collar and pocket in white
	1 hand in flesh
	1 crook in brown

Make up as for Humpty Dumpty and Soldiers.

Spider Glove Puppet
Mary Champion, Langport, Somerset

This knitted puppet is easy to make and operate, and could be amended to become an octopus.

Materials
50g DK wool
3¾mm (No 9) needles

Method
Cast on 36 stitches.
Rows 1–8: k2, p2.
Rows 9–12: st st.
Row 13 (thumb gusset): k17, inc in next st, k1, inc in next st, k16.
Row 14 and every alt row: p.
Row 15: k17, inc in next st, k3, inc in next st, k to end.
Continue to increase in this manner until there are 44 sts.
Division for thumb: k28, turn, p10, turn, cast on 2.
Work 18 rows in st st on these 12sts.
Next row: k2tog across row.
Next row: p2 tog across row. Thread wool through remaining sts and fasten off. Sew up seam.
With right side of work facing, pick up and k2sts at base of thumb, k sts across the back of glove.
Next row: p across all sts.
Work 6 rows in st st.

Fingers
1st finger: k23, turn, p10, turn, cast on 1st (11sts)
Work 18 rows st st. Finish off as thumb.
2nd finger: pick up and k1 at base of first finger, k5 turn, p10, turn, cast on 1st (11sts).
Work 18 rows st st. Finish as before.
3rd finger: pick up and k1 at base of second finger. K4, turn, p9, turn, cast on 1st (10sts).
18 rows st st. Finish as before.
4th finger: pick up and k2 from base of third finger, k remaining sts, turn, p all sts.
Work 18 rows st st. Finish as before. Sew up side seam.
Head. Make a woolly ball 45mm in diameter, stick or sew to back of glove.
Cut out small circles of white felt with smaller circles of black felt for the eyes. Stick the black on to the white and then stick to head for eyes. Add a strip of red felt to make a smiling mouth.

PUPPETS (opposite)

1 Choco the Clown (page 52)
2 Baby Hand Puppet (page 68)
3 Roland the Rat (page 70)
4 Snowman and Clown (page 71)
5 Sleeping Beauty's Castle (page 66)
6 Nursery Rhyme Finger Puppets (page 55)
7 Spider Glove Puppet (page 59)

DOLLS (overleaf)

1 Nightdress Case Doll (page 82)
2 Bustle Doll (page 76)
3 Penelope (page 73)
4 Pocket Polly (page 90)
5 Queenie Wood (page 79)
6 Lavender Handkerchief Doll (page 84)
7 Mini Doll (page 89)
8 Beanbag Mermaid (page 86)
9 Macramé Bead Dolls (page 91)
10 Lucy Lavender (page 88)
11 Granny Doll (page 87)

PRESENTS WITH A PURPOSE *(opposite)*

1 Book and Toy Holder *(page 102)*
2 Potato-Print Apron *(page 104)*
3 Cat and Mouse Writing Case *(page 94)*
4 A Storytime Cushion *(page 110)*
5 Bath-Time Panda and His Cuddly Twin *(page 106)*
6 Chicken Egg Cosy *(page 93)*
7 Miss Pinn *(page 110)*
8 Knitting Needle Case *(page 108)*
9 Sweet-Scented Pincushion *(page 108)*
10 Needlepoint Pincushion *(page 105)*

Sleeping Beauty's Castle with finger puppets
Marilyn Smith, Marlow, Bucks

This imaginative design contains a 'story book' of puppets, each 6.5cm high and made of felt. The 'doors' open out to form a scene 40×29cm worked in appliqué.

The Castle

Materials
2 pieces 10.5×30cm flower-patterned fabric
1 piece 21×30cm flower-patterned fabric
3 pieces wadding – sizes as above
2 pieces 10.5×30cm thin backing fabric
2 pieces 10.5×10cm blue fabric (sky)
2 pieces 10.5×10cm green-patterned fabric (grass)
2 pieces 10.5×25cm grey fabric (castle walls)
1 piece 21×30cm grey fabric (castle walls)
2 pieces 10×22cm slate-grey fabric (steps)
2 pieces 22×10cm purple, blue or red (throne)
oddments for bed, door and bushes
3m blue binding
trimmings
brown felt
press studs
NB The patterns give a 5mm seam allowance.

Making Up
Outside the castle
Take 2 pieces of flowered material 10.5×30cm, for the
  doors and 1 piece 30×21cm for the back.
Back each piece with wadding.
Zig-zag machine doors to simulate thorns; quilt back.

Inside castle grounds
1 Cut 2 pieces of thin backing material 10.5×30cm.
2 Sky. Cut 2 pieces of blue 10.5×10cm. Attach to
   backing flush with top.
3 Greenery. Cut 2 pieces of green 10.5×10cm. Attach
   to backing flush with bottom.
4 Castle walls. In grey cut 2 pieces as pattern (reverse

1) following complete outline. Transfer details to
   castle and machine or hand embroider. Appliqué to
   backing, covering bottom of sky and top of greenery.
5 Bush. Cut 2 in green as pattern and appliqué on to
   castle walls.
6 Join outside and inside doors together and bind
   edges with tape.

Inside the castle
1 Cut 1 piece 30×21cm in grey material.
2 Bed. Cut 2 headboards from pattern in plain
   material, machine right sides together leaving
   bottom open. Turn, press and sew to background.
   Cut 1 piece 8×10cm in pretty material for bed, turn
   in edges and sew to background leaving 4cm open in
   top side.
3 Pillow. Cut 1 piece 7×2.5cm, turn in edges and trim
   with lace. Sew into place stuffing lightly.
4 Bed cover. In same material cut 1 piece 6.5×10cm,
   turn in edges. Sew 3 sides over bed leaving the top
   open and the same 4cm opening as for bed. Stitch
   these openings together.
5 Door. Cut in dark grey or brown. Stitch woodwork
   and handle, and machine to background.
6 Steps. Cut 2 as pattern in slate grey. Machine steps
   at top edge only. Clip corners and turn, press and
   sew to background leaving 4cm open near door.
   (Other edges will be covered later.)
7 Throne. Cut 1 as pattern. Bind top edge to decorate,
   sew to background flush with bottom, covering
   bottom of steps and leaving 4cm open at top left-
   hand side. Suitable colours are red, blue or purple.
8 Throne seat. Cut in same material as throne,
   22×10cm. Fold lengthways and sew over lower part
   of throne leaving 2 openings 4cm long.
9 Join inside castle to flowered backing, trim and bind
   edges.
10 Position doors over the back so that they overlap in
   the centre. Join sides of doors to back. Sew press
   studs to centre opening.

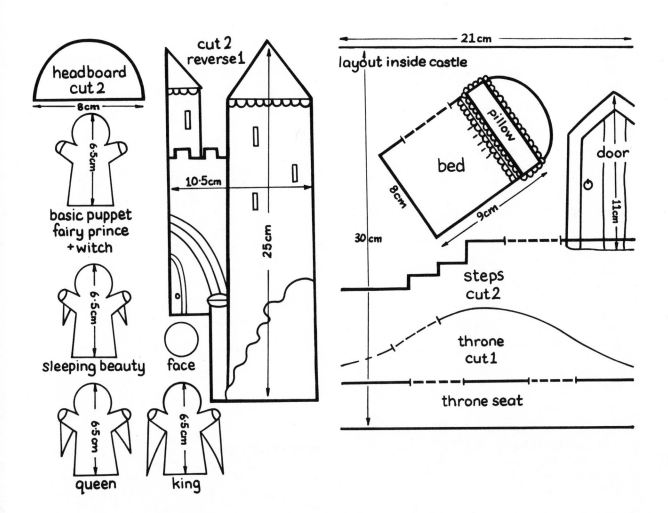

headboard
cut 2

8cm

6·5cm

basic puppet
fairy prince
+ witch

6·5cm

sleeping beauty

6·5cm

queen

6·5cm

king

face

cut 2
reverse 1

10·5cm

25 cm

21cm

layout inside castle

pillow

bed

8cm

9cm

door

11cm

30 cm

steps
cut 2

throne
cut 1

throne seat

Puppets

Materials
An assortment of small pieces of felt in yellow, red, green, blue, black, white, pink
wools for hair
embroidery cottons
glue

1 Using basic patterns cut 2 pieces in colour as directed.
   Sleeping Beauty – yellow   Prince – blue
   Queen – red   Witch – black
   King – green   Good Fairy – white or pale blue
2 Cut 1 pink face each and stick on except for Queen and Witch.
3 Cut 4 pink hands – sew over main colour.
4 Cut pieces as described below.

Sleeping Beauty
1 Cut 1 white collar and stick below head.
2 Embroider features on face.
3 Cut 16 pieces of black wool 8cm long and sew to head for hair.
4 Place in bed.

Queen
1 Cut 1 white back of head and collar.
2 Stick on face and embroider features.
3 Cut crown, decorate and stick to head.
4 Sew on hands.
5 Place in throne opening.

King
1 Embroider chain of office in French knots and beads.
2 Cut belt 6×0.5cm and stick on.
3 Cut hair and beard in black felt and stick on.
4 Embroider features.
5 Add crown decorated with beads.
6 Place in throne opening.

Prince
1 Embroider features and gold chain and belt.
2 Cut hat in mauve felt. Hat consists of a crescent-shaped front and 3 'feathers'. Sew feathers to top of hat so that they overlap each other.
3 Place in steps opening.

Fairy
1 Cut 16 pieces of gold wool into 8cm lengths for hair. Sew to head to cover back, catch at neck.
2 Make gold band with sequin at centre front.
3 Place fairy behind throne.

Witch
1 Cut white head and collar for front as for Queen.
2 Stick on face cut from beige felt with the top cut flat. Embroider.
3 Place behind bed.

Spinning wheel
1 Cut in brown felt and stitch spokes and thread in black.
2 Stick on background near bed.

Baby Hand Puppet
Ann Pollock, Newquay, Cornwall

Destined to capture many a heart, this baby puppet will provide plenty of scope for imaginative play and is easy to sew.

Materials
30×40cm acrilan fleece for blanket
45×20cm stretch towelling for doll's body (or old baby stretch suit)
small piece of flesh-coloured stockinette for head

12cm diameter circle of fur fabric for hair (or use wool)
wool to neaten edge of blanket
stuffing for head
20cm narrow lace
small piece of black felt for eyes (or use black embroidery thread)
red embroidery thread for mouth and nose
shirring elastic

Method

Body
1 Cut 2 body pieces.
2 Right sides together stitch all round body.
3 Carefully cut a slit in one piece of the body about 75cm long. Turn the doll right side out through the slit.
4 Run a gathering thread of shirring elastic loosely around the wrists and ankles.

Head
1 Cut out 2 heads.
2 Right sides together sew edges together leaving the base open. Turn right sides out.
3 Lightly stuff the head.
4 Put the head over the neck end of the puppet and sew together securely. (Keep a finger inside the neck piece so that you do not sew right through.)
5 Gather the lace to fit around the neck, and sew over the join between the head and body.
6 Run a gather thread 1cm inside the piece of fur fabric for hair and pull up to fit the doll's head. Sew on firmly.
7 Embroider the facial features or use felt. Make pink cheeks with crayon or lipstick. Seal the colour by pressing with a warm iron over a paper tissue.

Making Up
1 Blanket stitch edge of blanket with wool.
2 Cut a slit in the middle of blanket to match the slit in the doll.

3 Sew puppet to back of blanket, sewing round twice with an overstitch to make it firm.

Your puppet is now ready to use! Put your middle finger in the head, first and third fingers in the arms, thumb and little finger in the legs. Rest your puppet against your other arm.

enlarge × 2½

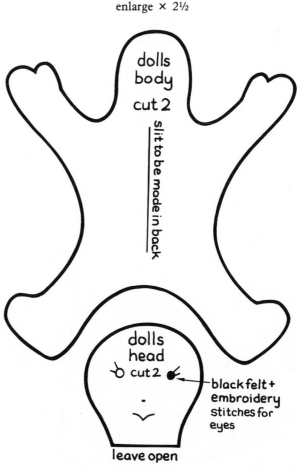

dolls body cut 2

slit to be made in back

dolls head cut 2

black felt + embroidery stitches for eyes

leave open

Roland the Rat

Sheila M. Wells, Neston, nr Corsham, Wilts

An interesting puppet; the basic shape – with amended nose and ears – could be made into a dog. 25cm high and made out of fabric, it is designed for a child.

Materials

30×60cm grey/brown/or white material (velvet looks good)
oddments of pink and black felt
2 black bead-like eyes
strong card (cereal packets are ideal)
glue
stuffing
4 lengths of nylon wire each 20cm long (fishing line will do)

Method

Body
1 Cut 2 body patterns. With right sides together machine up sides of body to points marked X on head. Zig-zag seams if frayable.
2 Turn under hem if frayable.

Ears
1 Cut 4 fabric outer ear pieces and 2 pink felt inner ear pieces.

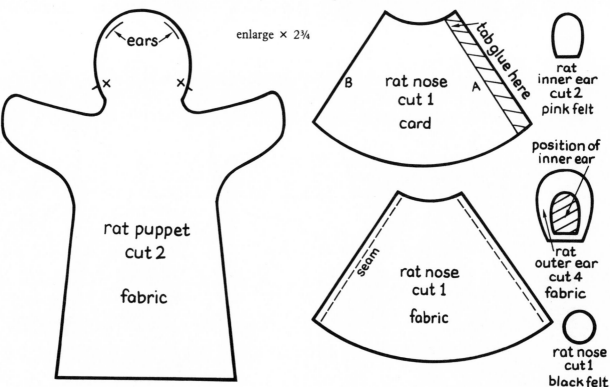

enlarge × 2¾

ears

×   ×

rat puppet
cut 2

fabric

tab glue here

B   rat nose
cut 1
card   A

rat
inner ear
cut 2
pink felt

position of
inner ear

seam

rat nose
cut 1
fabric

rat
outer ear
cut 4
fabric

rat nose
cut 1
black felt

70

2 With tiny stitches sew each pink inner ear to the right-side centre of an outer ear piece. Place the remaining outer ear pieces right sides down on top of these and machine with a very small stitch around the edges (6mm turning). Clip seams and turn right sides out.

3 Fold ears in half, with the pink pieces on the inside and pin to the right side of back of head, but pointing downwards in to the head. Make sure that the pink inner pieces are facing away from one another. Machine in place using a small stitch.

Nose

1 Cut nose out of card. Glue along tab and press to underside of B to make a cone.

2 Cut out fabric nose piece and fold in half (right sides together). Machine along side seam. Turn right side out.

3 Slide cardboard cone into nose piece until fitting snugly.

4 Cut black felt nose-tip and oversew on to tip of nose.

5 Using a needle, thread the whiskers through the end of the nose, taking them right through the cardboard, and fanning them out at different angles. On the inside of the nose spread plenty of strong glue over the area where the whiskers cross over, so that they cannot be pulled out.

6 With seam on the underside, position eyes (or sew on black felt circles) at broad end of nose.

7 Stuff nose generously.

Making up

1 Pin nose to right side front of head, tucking in the overlap of material from the nose. Oversew firmly in place, using double thread. Note that the nose covers almost the whole of the face.

2 Turn in the edges at the top of the head with small neat stitches.

Snowman and Clown
Elizabeth Horn, London SW1

Two puppets from the same basic design, easy to knit in stocking stitch and moss stitch.

Snowman

Materials
white and red balls of DK wool
3¼mm (No 10) needles
3 black buttons
black wool or embroidery thread

Method
Body (back and front alike)

1 Using 3¼mm needles cast on 32st in white
Row 1: * k1, p1, repeat from * to end
Row 2: * p1, k1, repeat from * to end
Rows 3, 5, 7: as row 1
Rows 4, 6: as row 2
Row 8: k
Row 9: p
Continue in st st
Rows 14, 21 and 28: dec 1 st at each end of row.

2 To shape sleeves:
Rows 36, 37: cast on 5 stitches at the beginning of row
Continue in st st but work the first and last 5 stitches of each row in moss stitch
Rows 45, 46: cast off 9st at beginning of each row.
Put remaining stitches on a holder.

3 Work front and back and join bodies at shoulders and sides, leaving hands open.

4 With right sides facing, put stitches on to 3 needles (12st on each needle). On each needle work:
Row 1: k2, k2tog, k4, k2tog, k2
Row 2: k
Row 3: inc 1 in next st, k13, inc 1 in next 2sts, k12, inc 1 in next st, k1

Row 4: inc 1 in next st, k15, inc 1 in next 2sts, k14,
   inc 1 in next st, k1
Row 5: inc 1 in next st, k17, inc 1 in next 2sts, k16,
   inc 1 in next st, k1
Row 6: inc 1 in 1st st, k19, inc in next 2sts, k19, inc
   1 in next st, k1
Rows 7-25: k
Row 26: *k1, k2tog, rep from *
Row 27: k
Row 28: k2tog to end
Row 29: k
Row 30: k2tog, k1, (k2tog) 5 times, k1, k2tog
Thread wool through stitches and fasten off inside.
5 Hat. With red wool cast on 60st
   Row 1: k
   Row 2: (k2tog, k1) to end
   Row 3: k
   Row 4: (k2tog, k2) to end (30st)
   Row 5: k
   Row 6: p
   Continue in st st for next 10 rows
   Cast off. Fold in half and join back and top seam.
6 Scarf. In red wool cast on 90st
   knit 6 rows
   cast off.
7 Sew hat and scarf on snowman, embroider face and
   add 3 black buttons to the front.

Clown

Materials
orange, white and brown DK wool
3¼mm (No 10) needles
red felt scraps
black wool or embroidery thread

Method
1 Work body as for snowman in colour with white
   head.
2 Hat. Cast on 40st in colour of body

Row 1: k
Row 2: (k2tog, k2) rep to end
Row 3: k
Row 4: p2tog, p11, (p2tog)twice, p11, p2tog
Row 5: k
Row 6: p
Row 7: k2tog, k9, (k2tog)twice, k9, k2tog
Row 8: p
Row 9: k
Row 10: p2tog, p7, (p2tog)twice, p7, p2tog
Row 11: k
Row 12: p
Row 13: k2tog, k5, (k2tog)twice, k5, k2tog
Row 14: p
Row 15: k2tog, k3, (k2tog)twice, k3, k2tog
Row 16: p
Row 17: k2tog, k1, (k2tog)twice, k1, k2tog
Row 18: (p2tog) 3 times
Finish by running thread through st and down side
   seam
Stitch hat to clown.
3 Make felt mouth and nose and embroider eyes. Add
   two contrasting bobbles on its front and a bell on the
   hat.

DOLLS *illustrated in colour on pages 62 and 63*

Penelope

Barbara Laberge, Canmore, Alberta, Canada

This beautiful doll stands 40cm high and is both elegant and cuddly. By using the same pattern but altering the facial features, hair style and clothes, you can produce a completely different-looking doll.

Materials

0.5m cotton poplin (body)
35g fluffy yarn (hair)
embroidery silks – red, blue, black, white, brown
powdered rouge (cheeks)
350g polyester stuffing
0.25m pink gingham (dress)
0.25m white cotton poplin (bloomers)
1 square white felt (shoes)
15cm ribbon broderie anglaise
1m ribbon broderie anglaise and ruffled trim combined
15cm broderie anglaise trim (bloomers)
1.5m pink ribbon (6mm wide)
elastic
3 small press studs
bias binding
fabric glue
2 small white or pearl beads (shoes)
small pearl beads (necklace)

Method

Seam allowances of 6mm are included on pattern pieces. Sew all body seams twice for extra strength. Clip all curves before turning (especially on head seams). Cut out body pattern pieces. Trace face lightly, with a pencil, on the right side of centre head section.

Face

1 Embroider mouth using one strand of red embroidery thread in satin stitch.
2 Embroider eyes in satin stitch using two strands of thread, use black for pupils, blue for iris, and white for the remainder (don't forget the white highlight on the pupils). In stem stitch using one strand of thread, embroider the eyebrows, nose, eye outline and eyelashes.
3 Start each section with a new piece of thread, otherwise thread may show through the fabric. For those who do not like embroidery the features may be painted, or drawn with waterproof pens.

Body

1 Stitch dart in centre front head. Slit back of head but do not stitch. Pin head sides to centre head and stitch.
2 With right sides together stitch body front and backs together leaving neck, back and bottom open. Turn to right side.
3 Pin and stitch head to neck. Turn head and body.
4 With right sides together stitch down the slit in the back of the head, continuing on down a portion of the back body.
5 Leave an opening as indicated on pattern, and stitch lower back bodies together.
6 Stitch leg pieces together, right sides together, leaving openings at the back for stuffing. Turn right side out.
7 Insert leg tops in the opening at the bottom of the body, and pin in place with toes pointing forward.
8 Push leg tops and corresponding fabric through the back body opening. Re-pin legs in position and sew together.
9 Pull legs out for stuffing.

Stuffing

1 Stuff using small pieces at a time to avoid hard lumps, using a crochet hook or a piece of dowelling to push stuffing into hands, thumbs and feet.
2 Stuff hands firmly and then arms up to within 10mm of sewing line as indicated on pattern. Sew on this line so that arms are moveable.
3 Stuff feet and legs to about 10mm from top of legs. With tiny overcast stitches, and double thread, sew up back openings.

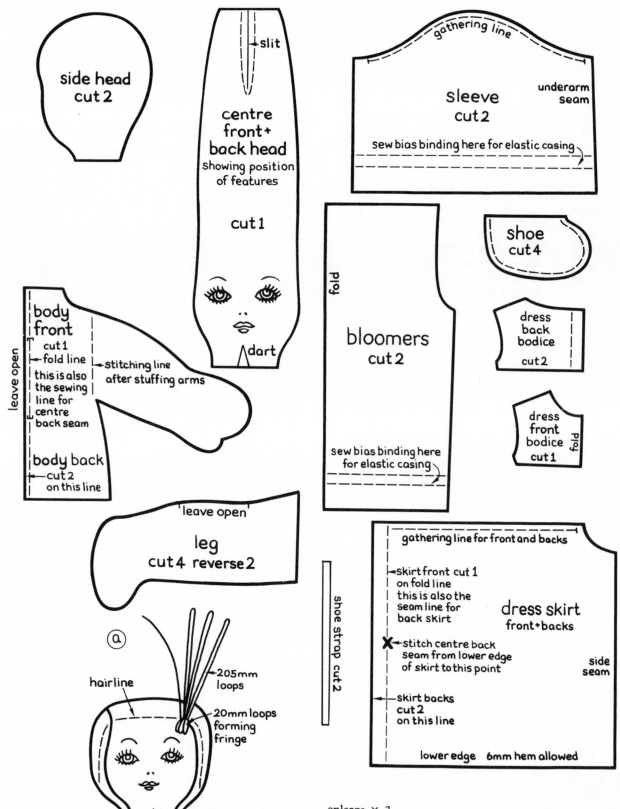

side head
cut 2

slit

centre
front +
back head
showing position
of features

cut 1

dart

gathering line

sleeve
cut 2

underarm
seam

sew bias binding here for elastic casing

shoe
cut 4

fold

bloomers
cut 2

sew bias binding here
for elastic casing

dress
back
bodice
cut 2

dress
front
bodice
cut 1

fold

body
front
cut 1
fold line
this is also
the sewing
line for
centre
back seam

leave open

stitching line
after stuffing arms

body back
cut 2
on this line

leave open

leg
cut 4 reverse 2

ⓐ

hairline

205mm
loops

20mm loops
forming
fringe

shoe strap cut 2

gathering line for front and backs

skirt front cut 1
on fold line
this is also the
seam line for
back skirt

✗ stitch centre back
seam from lower edge
of skirt to this point

skirt backs
cut 2
on this line

dress skirt
front + backs

side
seam

lower edge   6mm hem allowed

enlarge × 3

4 Stuff head and body very firmly through the back opening, making sure the neck and shoulders are well stuffed. Sew up back opening.

5 Brush rouge on the face for cheeks.

Hair

1 With a pencil, lightly draw hairline onto head, about 20mm above eyebrows, down sides of head, to about 10mm above the neck seam, (at back of head).

2 With matching thread sew yarn on to head. Do not cut yarn until hair is completed. Starting at the front, loop end of yarn about 20mm and sew to hairline; make another loop about 20cm long and again sew to hairline (a). Continue in this manner all around the hairline, making 'fringe' loops slightly shorter at the back of the neck. Cut yarn and secure thread.

3 Push hair away from head and cover head with fabric glue. Put hair back in place bringing the long loops together into a high ponytail. Tie securely with yarn. The ponytail may be trimmed or left as it is.

4 Tie piece of pink ribbon into a bow on ponytail.

Penelope's Outfit

6mm seam allowed on pattern pieces unless otherwise stated.

Dress

1 Cut out pattern pieces from gingham fabric.

2 Gather the upper edges of front and back as indicated on pattern. With right sides together pin and sew front bodice to front skirt and back bodice to back skirts. If necessary adjust gathers to fit before sewing.

3 Right sides together, stitch backs to front bodice at shoulder seams.

4 Thread a piece of pink ribbon through the ribbon broderie anglaise, pulling out enough in centre to tie in a bow. Pin and sew beading on front bodice.

5 Gather top of sleeves as indicated on pattern and pin to armhole edge. Sew seam.

6 Sew a piece of bias binding about 25mm from the sleeve edge. Measure elastic around doll's wrist, cut and thread through bias binding. Baste to keep in place.

7 With right sides together sew underarm seams and side seams.

8 Turn under about 6mm on sleeve edge and hem with small stitches.

9 Stitch centre back seam from bottom edge to X. Turn under and hem remaining back opening.

10 Cut piece of gingham crosswise, about 25mm wide and long enough to fit around neck. Right sides together, sew to neck edge. On inside of neck, hem the bias piece, neatening the edges at back of dress. Try dress on doll. Overlap one back edge over other, and place markers for press studs and sew on. Press dress.

11 Hem dress. On right side pin on bottom trim, thread ribbon through, then sew to dress, securing ribbon ends.

Bloomers

1 Cut pieces from poplin.

2 Right sides together, stitch centre front seam. Stitch leg seams. At top edge turn under 6mm and sew on bias binding. Measure elastic around doll's waist. Thread through bias binding, sew ends together and close opening.

3 At bottom of legs, turn under 6mm and sew on trim. Sew bias binding on wrong side of legs as indicated on pattern. Measure elastic around doll's legs. Thread through bias binding, sew ends together and close opening.

Shoes

1 Cut from white felt.

2 Stitch shoe pieces together. Sew strap to top of shoe overlapping strap at side of shoe. Sew on a small pearl bead to strap.

Dress doll and tie a string of pearls around her neck.

Bustle Doll

Diana Mountford, Southampton

This elegant doll is easy to make yet distinctly different and consequently she is a good fundraiser on a stall. Clothes and accessories can be made out of oddments while the body is a good way of using old tights. With a little practice any type of dress or period costume can be made.

Materials

1 wooden macramé bead for head
wire
0.75m fabric (main colour)
0.25m contrasting fabric
0.5m white cotton
pink nylon, or old tights
cotton for hair (brown/black/yellow, etc)
toning cotton for clothes
small long-nosed pliers
strong tape/fuse wire
ribbon (oddments)
1m lace or trim
glue
square of wood/balsa wood
clear varnish
jewellery or beads as required

Method

1 Using a short length of wire doubled, thread loop end through centre hole of bead and bend it over back of head. Twist strands of wire to form neck and bend ends outwards to form basis of shoulders (a).
2 Build rest of body as shown in (b), covering rough ends with fuse wire or tape.
3 Cut nylon or tights into strips 5cm wide and wind over frame, using extra padding to form bosom and bottom (c). Secure each length with stitching.
4 When desired shape is obtained, cover with wide piece of nylon or tights, securing neatly with small stitches at the back (d). (If using nylon, body can still be built with tights.) Cover legs first, then body. Do not do arms until hands are finished. Bend end of

legs up to form feet.
5 Hands. Cut tights into four 12×25mm strips. Roll into narrow 'sticks' and sew neatly. Cut two 18×25mm strips for thumbs and prepare in the same way.
6 Make up as shown in (e), bending two rolls to form four fingers.
7 Cover hands and arms in one single strip of nylon (with fingers hanging below), securing neatly at back and around and between fingers.
8 The completed basic doll shape can now be bent to any pose. The doll illustrated is approx 30cm high.

Clothes

1 Pantaloons: make as shown and attach to body (f).
2 Petticoat: cut in one piece, length measured from waist to ankle (g).
3 Skirt: cut as petticoat, leaving fullness to back. Add trim (h).
4 Under-bodice: cut strip to measure from under arm to just below waist (i). Add tiny beads for buttons.
5 Sleeves: sew onto bodice top and secure to doll (i).
6 Bustle: make small roll of material and secure to back of waist.
7 Over-skirt: cut material and gather top to fit back of waist, add trim and attach to doll over bustle (j).
8 Jacket: cut material to fit round top of doll leaving 2.5cm gap at front; attach sleeves. Skirt of jacket to reach just below shin (k). Attach to doll and trim as required (l).
9 Boots: cut from scrap of soft leather or felt, join and sew to doll (m).
10 Gloves: cut 2 glove shapes from felt or leather (to be attached to hand for decoration only).
11 Hat: cut shapes from card (n) and cover with material; attach crown to band and brim to band. Decorate with trim, rosettes made from gathered ribbon, and ribbons (n).
12 Hair: wind lengths of cotton between thumb and forefinger until roll is about 1in wide. Make several

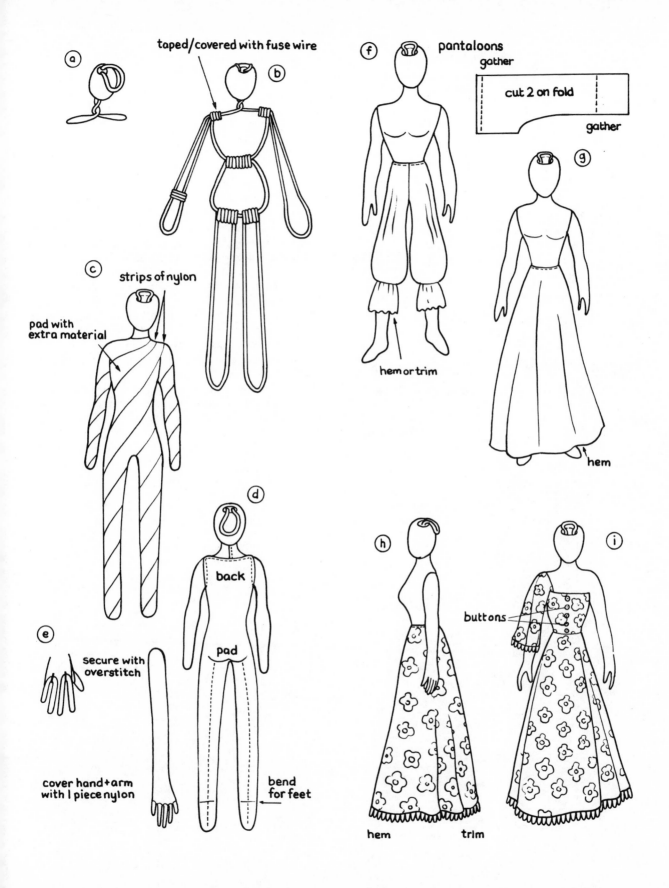

(a)

(b) taped/covered with fuse wire

(c) strips of nylon

pad with extra material

(d) back

pad

bend for feet

(e) secure with overstitch

cover hand+arm with 1 piece nylon

(f) pantaloons

gather

cut 2 on fold

gather

hem or trim

(g)

hem

(h) hem

(i) buttons

trim

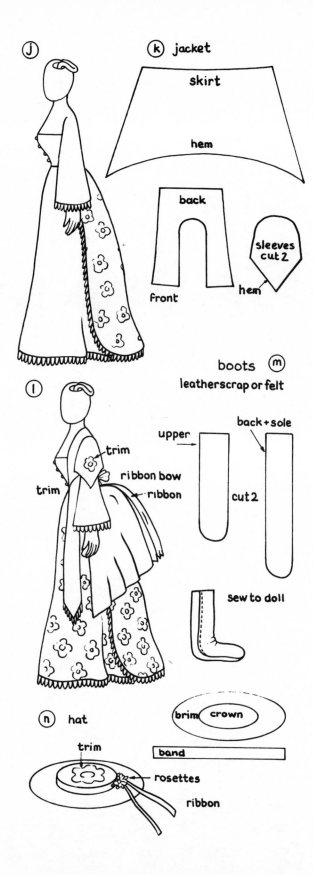

ⓙ

ⓚ jacket

skirt

hem

back

front

sleeves
cut 2

hem

boots ⓜ
leatherscrap or felt

ⓛ

trim

ribbon bow

trim

ribbon

upper

back + sole

cut 2

sew to doll

ⓝ hat

trim

brim crown

band

trim

rosettes

ribbon

rolls and sew to wire on top of head and secure at back until head is covered; glue under front pieces to secure. Make smaller roll of cotton to form bun and attach to top of head. Make 2 longer rolls, attach to either side of front parting, plait, take plaits around head and secure.

13 Face: cut tiny cone-shaped balsa-wood nose, glue to face, paint features with poster or acrylic paint, and cover face and hair with clear varnish.

14 Secure bonnet to head. Add any suitable jewellery or small trims as accessories.

15 Fix finished doll to wooden stand by hammering panel pins through feet and securing with glue. Stand can be painted or covered with fabric.

Queenie Wood

Marilyn A. Young, Hatfield, Herts

A knitted schoolgirl mascot doll to be proud of. Her clothes can be adapted to match any school uniform. She stands 35cm high. Queenie is the mascot of Queenswood School, Hatfield.

Materials

knitting needles: 1 pair 3¼mm (No 10); 1 pair 3mm (No 11); a stitch holder or an extra 3mm needle
1 × 25g ball of DK wool each in grey, beige, purple, and chosen hair colour
oddments in brown, white, and lilac
short lengths of fine wool for facial features
Sylko to match hair colour
1m ribbon 25mm wide
stuffing

Method

Feet (shoes) using 3mm needles and brown wool
1 Cast on 30sts; LSLW (for sewing up bottom of foot).
2 Work 8 rows in moss stitch, LSLW (for sewing up side of foot).

Socks
3 Join grey wool, LSLW
   st st 10 rows (beginning with a knit row).
4 Row 11: p
   Row 12: k (for mock turnover at top of socks).

Legs
5 Join flesh colour (beige), LSLW
   beginning with a k row, st st 16 rows.

Pants
6 Join grey wool, LSLW
   continue in st st working 8 rows.
7 Leave aside and repeat pattern making another leg to match.

8 Row 9: inc 1st each end of row (one leg). Place legs right sides together and tie end of wool to working wool. Continue knitting across the other leg, inc 1st at end of row (63 sts).
9 Continue in st st for another 11 rows (20 rows altogether of grey for pants). Leave aside on stitch holder or spare needle.

Skirt using 3¼mm needles and grey wool
10 Cast on 63 sts, LSLW.
11 First and alternate rows: k2, p1
    Second and alternate rows: k1, p2
    These two rows make the ribbing pattern. Knit into the back of the knit stitches. Work 26 rows (or 28 if a longer skirt is required).
    The skirt and pants are now joined together at the bottom of the jumper.

Jumper
12 With right side of both pieces (lower half of body and skirt) facing you, place skirt in front and on top of the body so that the skirt is now lying in place.
13 Tie the two grey ends of wool together, and then join purple wool. LSLW.
14 With a 3mm needle join lower half of body and the skirt at the waist by knitting through both lots of stitches together. Take the needle first through the skirt stitch and then the body stitch, wool round needle and pull wool through (63sts). This completes the first row of the jumper which is knitted in Fair Isle style.
15 st st 31 more rows using 3mm needles as below
    Rows 1–4: purple (pur)
    Rows 5, 6: white (w)
    Rows 7, 8: pur
    Rows 9, 10: w
    Rows 11–17: pur
    Shape V-neck as below
    Row 18: p: 31pur, 1w, 31pur
    Row 19: k: 30pur, 3w, 30pur

79

Row 20: p: 29pur, 2w, 1pur, 2w, 29pur
Row 21: k: 28pur, 2w, 3pur, 2w, 28pur
Row 22: p: 27pur, 2w, 2pur, 1w, 2pur, 2w, 27pur
Row 23: k: 26pur, 2w, 2pur, 3w, 2pur, 2w, 26pur
Row 24: p: 25pur, 2w, 2pur, 2w, 1pur, 2w, 2pur, 2w, 25pur
Row 25: k: 24pur, 2w, 2pur, 2w, 3pur, 2w, 2pur, 2w, 24pur
Row 26: p: 23pur, 2w, 2pur, 2w, 5pur, 2w, 2pur, 2w, 23pur
Row 27: k: 22pur, 2w, 2pur, 2w, 3pur, 1lil, 3pur, 2w, 2pur, 2w, 22pur
Row 28: p: 21pur, 2w, 2pur, 2w, 3pur, 3lil, 3pur, 2w, 2pur, 2w, 21pur
Row 29: k: 20pur, 2w, 2pur, 2w, 3pur, 5lil, 3pur, 2w, 2pur, 2w, 20pur
Row 30: p: 19pur, 2w, 2pur, 2w, 3pur, 7lil, 3pur, 2w, 2pur, 2w, 19pur
Row 31: k: 18pur, 2w, 2pur, 2w, 3pur, 9lil, 3pur, 2w, 2pur, 2w, 18pur
Row 32: p: 17pur, 2w, 2pur, 2w, 3pur, 11lil, 3pur, 2w, 2pur, 2w, 17pur

Note: It may be found easier to keep the shaping of the V-neck of the jumper more even if a length of the white and the lilac wool are each threaded through a sewing needle, and the wool carried by passing each sewing needle through the loop below the stitch next door but one before the stitch about to be knitted in the new colour (on the wrong side). With the white wool this should be done from row 19 to the last row of the jumper inclusive. With the lilac wool this should be done from row 28 to the last row of the jumper inclusive.

Face
16 Join flesh colour (beige), LSLW
 work 16 rows in st st.

Head
17 Join hair colour and shape head as follows (63sts):
 Row 1: k6, k2tog, k12, k2tog, k19, k2tog, k12, k2tog, k6 (59sts)
Row 2 and alternate rows: p
Row 3: k7, k2tog, k11, k2tog, k15, k2tog, k11, k2tog, k7 (55sts)
Row 5: k6, k2tog, k12, k2tog, k11, k2tog, k12, k2tog, k6 (51sts)
Row 7: k5, k2tog, k12, k2tog, k9, k2tog, k12, k2tog, k5 (47sts)
Row 9: k4, k2tog, k11, k2tog, k9, k2tog, k11, k2tog, k4 (43sts)
Row 11: k4, k2tog, k9, k2tog, k9, k2tog, k9, k2tog, k4 (39sts)
Row 13: k2, k2tog, k9, k2tog, k9, k2tog, k9, k2tog, k2 (35sts)
Row 15: k3, k2tog, k6, k2tog, k9, k2tog, k6, k2tog, k3 (31sts)
Row 17: k1, k2tog(7times), k1, k2tog(7times), k1 (17sts)
18 LSLW. Thread wool through a sewing needle and take the wool through the remaining stitches.

Arms with 3mm needles and purple wool
19 Cast on 8sts LSLW (for sewing arm to body).
20 st st as follows:
 Row 1: k (k into the back of sts of this row)
 Row 2: p, inc 1st at each end of row
 Rows 3–9: inc 1st each end of row (24sts).
21 Continuing in st st:
 21 rows pur
 2 rows w
 2 rows pur
 2 rows w
 4 rows pur, LSLW.

Hands in beige
22 st st 8 rows
 dec row: k2tog(12times) (12sts), LSLW.
23 Thread wool through sewing needle and take wool through remaining stitches.
24 Make another arm to match.

To make up

1 Finish off ends with a sewing needle or a crochet hook (except for those that have been left for sewing up).

2 With warm iron, lightly press pieces on the wrong side of the knitting using a damp cloth. Avoid ironing moss stitch, ribbing, and the top of the socks.

3 Sewing up. Oversew moss stitch and ribbing. Back stitch st st. Allowing turnings of 6mm.

4 Fold doll lengthwise inside out and begin by sewing up the skirt. Oversew both up and down the skirt.

5 Push skirt into upper half of doll out of the way and sew up the sides of the feet and legs. Leave the bottom of the feet open until stuffing is completed.

6 Pants. Sew seams (continuation of leg seams) as far as crotch. Sew from crotch to waist.

7 Sew up the jumper. Great care is needed to make sure that the stripes meet neatly at the back.

8 Sew up the face leaving the head open for stuffing.

9 Turn right side out.

10 Fold each arm lengthwise inside out, pull hand thread tight and sew up hand.

11 Sew up arm leaving the top open for stuffing (make sure the stripes meet neatly). Turn right side out.

12 Stuffing. Stuff from the top making sure that all extremities are well stuffed.

13 Pull head thread tight and sew up the head. Sew up the bottoms of the feet.

14 Neck-cord. Thread a length of flesh-coloured wool through a needle, and run it through the knitting round the neck, leaving the two ends long enough to pull. Pull the ends to shape the neck. Tie the ends tightly, take each end through the doll, and cut carefully.

15 Do the same with the ankles using grey wool.

16 Sew arms to body.

17 De-fluff the doll by dabbing a strip of Sellotape over it to remove unwanted fluff.

18 Hair (plaits). With the back of the doll facing you, make the hair foundation line for the parting (see diagram) which consists of 3 long visible stitches: 1) up the back of the head, 2) across the top, 3) from the top of the head to the edge of the hair line in front. The two ends are left showing at the side of the face until the plaits are completed as it is sometimes necessary to pull the ends tighter. These will be cut off afterwards.

19 Cut 78 pieces of wool 70cm long of chosen hair colour.

20 Each piece of hair is threaded through a needle and taken either side of the foundation thread into the knitting of the doll.

21 Start at the back of the hair just above the beginning of the neck and tie each piece of hair in place with an overhand knot. Continue until the whole foundation thread is covered.

22 Divide each side of hair into three and plait. Bind each plait about 40mm from the end with Sylko.

23 Cut away hair foundation ends.

24 Cut 2 ribbons each 40cm long and tie a bow on each plait. Trim plaits and bows.

25 Face. Embroider the eyes and mouth.

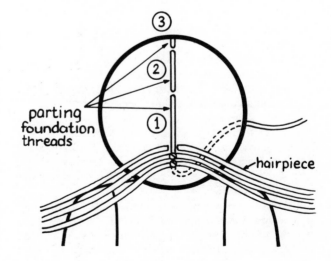

Nightdress Case Doll

Susan L. Wilkes, Sale, Cheshire

This lovely doll doubles as a nightdress case or tidy bag and the design is based on 'There was a little girl who had a little curl'. She appeals to young and old alike. She is 60cm long with a skirt large enough to take an adult's nightdress. The dress can easily be removed for washing.

Materials
1m flowered cotton fabric
0.5m white fabric
40×22cm flesh-coloured felt
scraps of pink and black felt
30cm zip (or press studs can be used)
press studs
thick wool for hair
ribbon for hair
stuffing
lace for trimming
embroidery silks

Method

Doll
1 Body. Cut 2 body patterns out of the felt. Sew the darts.
2 Machine round side and head leaving the base open (a 3mm seam allowance is given). Turn to right side and stuff firmly. Sew bottom opening securely. Tie a thread securely round doll's neck.
3 Sew and glue on features.
4 Take 9 strands of thick wool 60cm long and sew them to the centre of the head. Sew a few extra loops here for her curl. Take the strands down either side of the head and secure at neck. Plait the remainder and trim off neatly.
5 Arms. Same method as for body. Stuff only half way up and sew a few stitches through the arm to prevent the stuffing from moving. Sew the arms to the body 2.5cm down from the neck.

Hat
1 Cut 2 circles of flowered fabric 30cm diameter. With right sides together sew round leaving a small opening. Turn right side out and trim with lace.
2 Run a gathering thread 4cm from the outer edge and draw up to fit back of head. Place a little stuffing in hat and sew to head.

Dress
Bodice
1 Sew shoulder seams of bodice and bodice lining.
2 Place bodice and bodice lining right sides together and sew back, neck and sides. Clip curves round neck. Turn right side out and press.
3 Hem sleeves and trim with lace.
4 Sew sleeve seam. Gather top of sleeve and sew to bodice. Turn right side out.

Skirt
1 Cut a piece of material 45×90cm.
2 Sew lace 4cm from one long edge. This is the bottom.
3 Run a gathering thread around the top, gather and fix to bodice, with opening at centre back.
4 Hem each short edge to give an opening 30cm from the waist. Right sides together machine remainder of back seam and bottom of bag.
5 Insert zipper in skirt or sew on press studs.
6 Sew 2 press studs on bodice.
7 Make a rosette of lace and sew to front of dress.

Apron
1 Cut a piece of white material 27×40cm and hem around 2 short and 1 long edge.
2 Sew 2 rows of lace along long hemmed edge.
3 Gather other long edge to 14cm.
4 Cut waistband 28×3cm.
5 Turn in a narrow edge all the way round waistband. Fold in half and sew enclosing apron front 6cm in from either end. Sew on a press stud.

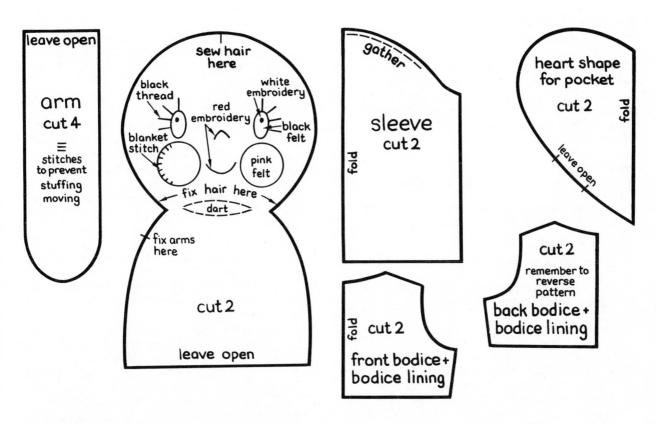

6 Shoulder straps. Cut two 13 × 3cm.
7 Press in narrow turning along long edges. Fold in half and machine, trimming with lace.
8 Sew straps to back of waistband near centre front and back.
9 Pocket. Cut 2 heart shapes as pattern.
10 Right sides together machine edges leaving small opening.
11 Turn right sides out and press. Sew to apron.

Dress doll and tie on hair ribbons. To hang up tie narrow ribbon around neck.

enlarge × 2¼

Lavender Handkerchief Doll

Eileen M. Roberts, Wimborne, Dorset

A lavender doll with a difference. This little doll is easy to make, smells delightful and is a doubly useful gift – pull out the pins, cut the gathering thread around the skirt and you have a novel way of sending two handkerchiefs. The ribbon round the doll's neck can be looped and hung in a wardrobe. Height 19cm.

Materials

2 pieces of fine cotton lawn 25cm sq (or purchase ready made handkerchiefs)
oddments of fine gauge nylon (or similar fine material which will allow lavender smell to penetrate)
2m of narrow lace
small length of ribbon
embroidery threads (use two threads) and small motif
small amount of 4-ply brown wool for hair
10 × 36cm woven interfacing for underskirt
small piece of felt or material for face
sewing cotton
35g dried lavender

Method

(NB All gathering thread should be double cotton. 10mm seam allowance on all pieces.)

1 Cut out the body, head, legs and arms in fine gauge material (if material is very fine use double thickness).
2 Sew body, legs and arms along bottom and sides, leaving tops open for stuffing. Stitch seams securely; if machining use stretch stitch (a).
3 Trim seams and turn to right side.
4 Fill with lavender fairly tightly.
5 Turn in top edges of arms and legs and oversew.
6 Head. Cut circle of fine gauge material 12cm diameter and run gathering thread 15mm from the edge (b). Fill with lavender, at the same time drawing up thread to make a round ball shape. Pack lavender tightly and fasten off securely.
7 Turn in top of body and run gathering thread all round. Place gathered edge of head inside top of body and draw up body thread tightly to fit neck of head (c). Secure head to body by stitching all round neck edge (c).
8 Sew arms and legs on to body, legs folded with seam in front and stitched flat (c).
9 Hair. Wind wool loosely round a piece of card the required size, slide off and place on paper (d). Stitch 2 rows through the middle to secure, remove paper.
10 Make face from felt or suitable material. Either embroider or mark facial features and stitch to head.
11 Place hair with stitching on top of head and secure. Trim to required length.

To dress doll

1 Make small top if desired (e), using fine material which does not fray.
2 Stitch back seam of stiffened underskirt, gather top edge and draw up to fit doll's waist, secure to body with a few stitches.
3 Handkerchiefs may be made from cotton lawn entirely as desired. (Originals were hand hemstitched with drawn threads, one white, one coloured.) Embroider small motif in corner of one, and stitch lace around all edges.
4 Skirt. Fold handkerchiefs as shown (f), run a gathering thread along the top and draw up to fit the waist.
5 Cloak. Place middle of one edge of handkerchief at top of head, bring round sides of head securing in place with a ribbon tied in a bow round the neck. Allow the two corners to fall in front of doll, take adjoining edges and bring them up behind and under the arms and fasten corners and edges in middle of doll just above the skirt. The surplus at the back of the doll is carefully folded and pleated and secured with pins or stitches.

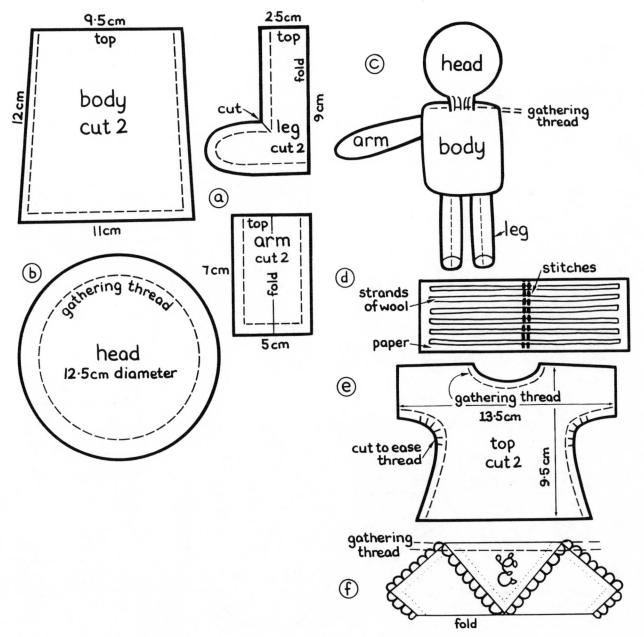

9.5 cm

top

12 cm

body
cut 2

11 cm

(a)

2.5 cm

top

fold

cut

leg
cut 2

9 cm

(b)

gathering thread

head
12.5 cm diameter

top

arm
cut 2

fold

7 cm

5 cm

(c)

head

arm

body

= = gathering
thread

leg

(d)

strands
of wool

stitches

paper

(e)

gathering thread

13.5 cm

cut to ease
thread

top
cut 2

9.5 cm

(f)

gathering
thread

fold

85

Beanbag Mermaid

Heather Eburne, Great Baddow, Chelmsford

An unusual doll for any collection; 20cm high, simple and cheap to make, it can be adapted to make an ordinary soft toy by substituting stuffing for the beans.

Materials
30 × 12cm flesh-coloured material
18 × 12cm green material (use non-fray fabrics)
scraps of felt for eyes and flower
yellow wool
4tbsp dried beans (or split peas) and small ball of stuffing
fabric glue
scrap of lace

Method
1 Cut front and back body out of flesh-coloured material, front and back tail and pattern A out of green-coloured material (a 5mm seam allowance is given).
2 Sew curved edge of A to top curved edge of back tail (which when opened out will form mermaid's 'seat' and allow her to sit up). Then sew straight edge of A piece to straight edge of back body.
3 Sew straight edges of front tail and body together at waist. Then pin complete body pieces right sides together and sew all round, leaving gap at top of head for split peas and stuffing. Turn right side out.
4 Fill with split peas (about 4tbsp to allow for movement).
5 Run gathering thread around neck, pull tightly, wrap thread a few times around neck and fasten off.
6 Fill head to a nice rounded shape with stuffing. Oversew gap in top of head.
7 Cut 25 25cm lengths of wool, and sew centre across top of head. Catch strands to each side of head just above neck and sew. Trim hair to even length.
8 Cut small circles of black felt for eyes and glue to face. Embroider nose and mouth. Colour cheeks by rubbing lightly with red crayon.
9 Sew scraps of lace for sea shells on to mermaid's chest.

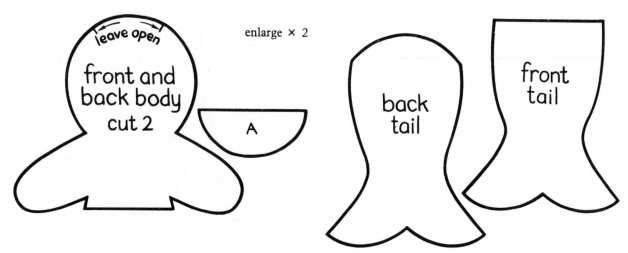

enlarge × 2

86

Granny Doll

Irene Hill, Mexborough, S Yorks

This is a soft-bodied doll with a plaster of Paris face. Details are given below for making the head. Different clothes and accessories can be substituted, of course.

Materials

celluloid doll mask (imprint must go through to the back of the face)
plaster of Paris or dental plaster
paints
cotton wool or wool for hair

Method

Face
1   Fill mould with water and then pour into a plastic container such as a margarine carton.
2   Gently shake in enough plaster of Paris to come just below the surface. Leave to stand for a short while if using dental powder, a little longer if using plaster of Paris.
3   Stir gently. Pour into face mask and allow to dry.
4   Gently ease edges of mask away from the sides. Turn over and tap into palm of hand.
5   When completely dry paint the face. Matt paint is used here but any paint can be used provided that, if the doll is for a child, the paints are completely safe.

Hair
The simplest and best way of making a granny doll's hair is to use cotton wool. If a bubbly curl is required, the hair can be knitted as follows:
1   Cast on enough stitches to frame the face of the doll.
    Row 1: insert needle into first stitch, wind wool 4 times round needle and first finger and take over first st. With 4 sts now on right-hand needle, put other needle through sts and knit together. Repeat to end of row.

Row 2: knit.
    These two rows form the pattern.
2   Gradually decrease sts at each end of knit rows to shape the back of the head. If the hair-piece is slightly large, so much the better, as the hair will appear thicker.
3   Glue the front of the hair-piece round the face. Allow to dry then glue from top of head to neck. Glue the two loose sides last of all.

Now dress the doll as you wish – baby, child, adult, granny, period doll – the choice is endless.

Lucy Lavender

Susan A. Burton, Trowbridge, Wilts

Everyone from grandma to tiny tots will love squeezing this doll and releasing her delightful lavender aroma. She is quick and easy to make and is an ideal present to send through the post. She is 15cm high.

Materials

2 15cm squares of flesh-coloured felt
4-ply wool oddment for hair
small scrap of felt for eyes
20 × 10cm cotton fabric for dress
50cm lace (20mm wide)
sewing thread
dried lavender
glue
short length of shirring elastic

Method

The Doll

1   Trace the pattern on to tracing or greaseproof paper. Pin pattern on to the two layers of felt.
2   Machine stitch round, close to the edge leaving the top of the head open for filling, as shown on pattern. Cut out doll close to stitching line.
3   Fill the doll with dried lavender and then close opening.
4   Cut 50 12cm lengths of 4-ply wool and attach centre of strands to top of head with a line of stitching. 'Layer cut' hair a little to make it hang attractively. Spread the back and sides of head with a little glue and press hair down to secure.
5   Cut two circles of suitably coloured felt (1cm diameter) for eyes. Glue in position.
6   Embroider mouth.

enlarge × 2

88

Clothes

1 Cut 11cm of lace for panties. Join raw edges with a 5mm seam to form a tube. Slide on to doll's body. Catch together between legs with a few small stitches.

2 Dress. Take 2 10×10cm squares of cotton fabric. With right sides together stitch up side seams to within 5cm of the top edge (5mm seam allowance allowed).

3 Make a narrow hem along the two top and the bottom edges (1cm allowed).

4 Using a needle, thread a short length of shirring elastic through the top edges of the dress.

5 Draw up to fit doll's neck and knot securely.

6 Cut 2 9cm lengths of lace and catch along neck edge, back and front.

7 Stitch lace in position around hem.

Mini Doll

Alison Riley, Hinckley, Leics

Delightfully simple, this little doll – only 15cm high – can be made from scraps of felt and fabric to produce a charming little gift.

Materials

pieces of flesh-coloured felt
scraps of printed cotton fabric
stuffing
brown DK wool
small piece of black felt
red embroidery thread
scraps of lace trimming
ribbon bow
clear adhesive

Method

1 For the head, cut a 10cm diameter circle of flesh-coloured felt. Run a gathering thread around the edge. Pull up gathers, stuff firmly and fasten off. Mould this ball into a head shape, making sure that the gathers are at the back.

2 For the eyes, cut two small ovals of black felt and glue in place.

3 Work the nose and mouth in red thread, taking the stitches to the back of the head to secure.

4 For the hair, wind the yarn three times around your little finger and stitch the loops in place. Take the hair around the face and across the back of the head. Secure all the loops to the head with small stitches.

5 For the body, cut a 10×12cm piece of felt. Join the two short edges.

6 For the base, cut a 4cm diameter circle of felt. Sew in place at one open end of the body. Turn right side out.

7 Stuff firmly to within about 2cm of the top edge. Gather this edge tightly and sew to the head with ladder stitch.

8 For the dress, cut a 11×15cm piece of fabric. Hem one long edge and sew on lace trimming. With right sides together, join the two short sides. Turn right sides out. Turn in and gather the remaining raw edge and stitch to the doll's neck distributing the gathers evenly.

9 For each arm, cut a piece of fabric 5×6.5cm. Fold in raw edges on one short end. Fold fabric in half and join the long edges. Turn right sides out.

10 Cut hand from felt and glue into neatened end of arm. Stuff arm lightly. Turn in and gather remaining raw edges of arm and sew in position at the side of the body, just under the neck.

11 For the hat, cut two 15cm diameter circles of fabric. With right sides together, sew around the edge, leaving a gap for turning. Turn right side out. Ladder stitch opening. Run a gathering thread 2cm from the outer edge. Pull up gathers to fit the head, fasten off. Stuff the crown of hat lightly. Sew hat to head.

12 Glue a ribbon bow to the neck at front.

Pocket Polly

Val Davies, Glasgow

*A 'baby' doll 19cm high, ready for, and equipped with, bed!
Simple to sew yet fun to own.*

Materials

50×20cm cotton fabric for doll
small ball of wool for hair
embroidery silks for features
stuffing
30×20cm cotton fabric for nightdress
trimming for neck and sleeves
press stud
45×25cm quilted fabric for pocket
trimming
1m braid

Method

Doll

1 Cut out 2 doll shapes and sew the halves together
   with a 5mm seam allowance; leave a gap across the
   top of the head. Carefully snip all corners and turn
   material to right side.
2 Stuff the doll and sew up head seam.
3 Embroider facial features (a).
4 Hair. Cut wool into 23cm lengths – about 40 lengths
   if using poodle wool. Beginning at forehead and
   allowing wool to hang over face and down to eyes –
   about 4cm (a) – stitch firmly from A to B. Gather the
   wool together at back of neck to cover about 25mm
   and stitch firmly from C to D (b). Lift centre 12
   lengths of wool back to the top of the head and stitch
   over the A to B line (c). The 14 lengths left at either
   side of the neck are each lifted up the side of the head
   and stitched in a bunch at each end of the A to B
   stitching line (d). The remaining wool then hangs
   down the side of the head. Trim fringe and hair
   carefully (d).

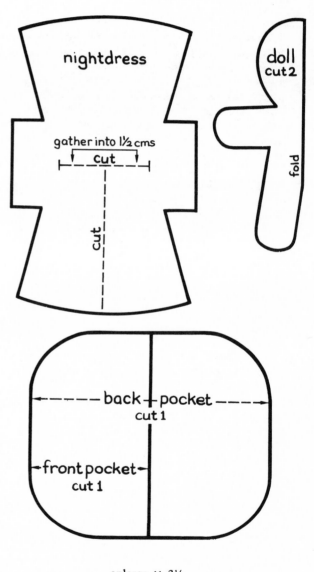

enlarge × 3½

Nightdress

1 Gather front neck edge as shown on pattern.
2 Hem neck edge and sleeve edge and trim with narrow lace.
3 Hem back opening edges and sew fastener at neck edge.
4 Fold at shoulders, right sides together, and sew underarm and side seams.
5 Hem bottom edge.

Pocket

1 Turn over top edge of front pocket piece and trim with lace or embroidery remnant.
2 Place front pocket piece on back pocket piece, right sides up, and tack together.
3 Pin braid right round edge of pocket, tack and sew (e).
4 Pop Polly in her pocket.

Macramé Bead Dolls

Rhoda Johnson, Wroughton, Wilts

It is easy to make a collection of these little people. They are simple and cheap to make and have the advantage of standing upright. At 8cm high they would be suitable for a doll's house.

Materials

2 macramé beads (a), brown or natural colour
14cm long pipe cleaner
8cm long pipe cleaner
2 × 15mm lengths of corset lace or brown shoe lace
oddments of small patterned material
lace and ribbon for decoration
paper tissue
a little wallpaper paste
red, black and brown paint

Method

1 Fold the 8cm pipe cleaner into four and glue one end into a round bead for the head and neck.
2 Soak paper tissue in wallpaper paste and model hair on head. Leave in a warm place until thoroughly dry.
3 Paint hair on brown bead black, on natural bead brown. Paint eyes black, mouth red (b).
4 Glue a piece of corset or shoe lace over each end of

91

14cm pipe cleaner leaving half extending beyond
cleaner. Put glue inside loose end and press flat.
When dry shape to form hands.

5 Wind cleaner round top of long bead to form arms
  and glue into place (c).
6 From flowered material cut skirt 16 × 5cm and bodice
  (d).
7 Fold bodice wrong side out matching letters, and
  stitch side seams, turn right side out and put on to
  body and arms.
8 Glue neck piece of head into hole in top of body.
9 Gather sleeve ends and stitch to wrists; trim with
  lace.
10 Join short sides of skirt, neaten one long edge and
   trim with lace. Turn under narrow hem on other
   long edge, gather and stitch to waist of doll.
11 Make sash from ribbon and stitch to dress.

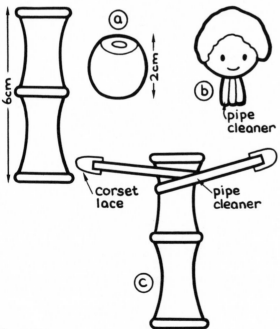

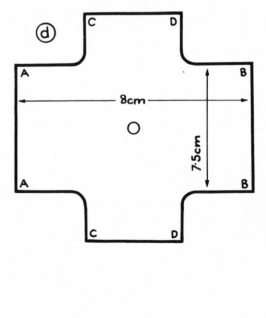

PRESENTS WITH A PURPOSE *illustrated in colour on page 64*

Chicken Egg Cosy
Margaret A. Brown, Lechlade, Glos

To brighten your breakfast table, simple to make and crocheted in 4-ply.

Materials
oddments of yellow, orange, green, white and red 4-ply
3.5 crochet hook

Method
In yellow, make 16ch, ss into first ch to form ring.

Round 1: 1ch, 1dc into each ch of ring, ss into first ch of this round.

Round 2: 1ch, 3dc into next dc, 1dc into each dc to end of round, ss into 1ch at beg of round.

Round 3: 1ch, 1dc into each dc to end, ss into 1ch at beg of round.

Round 4: 1ch, 1dc into first dc, 3dc into next dc, 1dc into each of next 9dc, 2dc into next dc, 1dc into each of next 7dc, ss into 1ch at beg of round.

Rounds 5, 7, 9, 11, 13, 14: as round 3.

Round 6: 1ch, 1dc into next 2dc, 3dc into next dc, 1dc into each dc to end, ss into 1ch at beg of round.

Round 8: 1ch, 1dc into next 3dc, 3dc into next dc, 1dc into each dc to end, ss into 1ch at beg of round.

Round 10: 1ch, 1dc into next 4dc, 3dc into next dc, 1dc into next 13dc, 2dc into next dc, 1dc into next 7dc, ss into 1ch at beg of round.

Round 12: 1ch, 1dc into next 5dc, 3dc into next dc, 1dc into next 14dc, 2dc into next dc, 1dc into next 8dc, ss into 1ch at beg of round.

Round 15: ss into next 3dc, 1ch, 1tr into each of next 3dc, 2tr into each of next 2dc, 1tr into each of next 3dc, 1dc into each dc to end working over the 3ss at beg of round, ss into 1ch at beg of round and change colour of yarn.

Round 16 (orange): ss into first tr, 2ch 2tr into same place as ss, 3tr into each of next 9tr, 1dc into each dc to end, ss into 2nd of 2ch at beg of round and change

colour of yarn.

Round 17 (green): 2ch and 1tr into same place as ss, 2tr into each of next 29tr, 1dc into each dc to end, ss into 2nd of 2ch at beg of round and change colour of yarn.

Round 18 (white): 2ch, 1tr into each of next 58tr, 1dc into each dc to end, ss into 2nd of 2ch at beg of round and change colour.

Edging (red): (1dc into next tr, 2ch) repeat 57 times, 1dc into next tr, 1dc into each dc to end. Fasten off.

Beak (red): Rejoin yarn 1cm from cast-on edge and work 2ch 2tr and 1dc into same place as join. Fasten off.

Comb (red): Join yarn to cast-on edge. Work 7dc along edge through double fabric. Turn, * 2ch, ss into space between dc*, repeat from * to * to end. Fasten off.

Embroider eyes in brown through double fabric.

Cat and Mouse Writing Case
Stella Smith, Johannesburg, S Africa

A present that will please both young and old – worked in felt and embroidery on fabric. The case measures 22.5 × 25cm. Inside there is a place for a writing pad, envelopes and pen.

Materials
1m sky-blue even-weave linen 58cm wide
1 × 1m thin cardboard
scraps of felt in red, canary yellow, mustard yellow, black and white
1 skein shaded yellow stranded embroidery cotton
small quantities red, sky-blue and black stranded embroidery cotton
1 reel sky-blue sewing cotton
coloured paper or wall-paper for motifs
glue
blue writing pad and envelopes
blue ball-point pen

Method

Front and back covers
1 Cut 4 pieces 24 × 27cm of even-weave linen.
2 On one piece trace picture of cat sitting among flowers. Work according to pattern. When completed, iron from wrong side on to folded towel.
3 From sheet of cardboard cut 4 pieces 22 × 25cm.
4 Cover one side of each piece of cardboard with piece of the linen, including worked piece, and fold over excess material to other side. With cardboard facing, sandwich these together in pairs and oversew edges.

Envelope pocket
1 Cut piece of cardboard 9 × 19cm (a). Score lightly along dotted lines, snip bottom corners on solid lines and fold back. Glue corner overlaps together.
2 Cut piece of linen 11 × 21cm. Cover outside of folded cardboard, folding excess material to other side and gluing the edge of the material to the cardboard.

94

Fold the material neatly at the corners and secure with a few stitches.
3 Position the pocket on inside of front cover with bottom edge of pocket 7cm from lower edge of cover and slightly to the right of centre. Stitch pocket to cover along three touching sides.

Loops for ball-point pen
1 Cut 2 pieces of linen 3 × 4cm. Turn in 1cm all round. Oversew two long sides of each piece.
2 Position both loops on inside of front cover 5cm above envelope pocket and 5cm apart. With seam touching cover, stitch each loop down 5mm along either side of seam.

Strip for writing pad
1 Cut piece of cardboard 5 × 20cm.
2 Cut piece of linen 12 × 22cm.
3 Turn in linen 1cm all round and cover cardboard completely. Oversew both ends and two long sides with seam running along back of cardboard.
4 Position strip on inside of back cover 5cm from upper edge of cover. Stitch two short ends to cover.

Spine
1 Cut piece of cardboard 3 × 25cm.
2 Cut piece of linen 8 × 27cm.
3 Turn in linen 1cm all round and cover cardboard completely. Oversew both ends and two long sides with seam running along one long edge of cardboard.
3 Using three strands of sky-blue embroidery thread, herringbone spine to inner edges of front and back cover.

Motifs for writing pad
1 Trace motifs (b and c) on coloured paper or wall-paper, keeping to colour scheme used on front cover. Cut out and stick on to each sheet of writing pad. The arrangement and colours of motifs can be varied. Motifs illustrated are actual size.

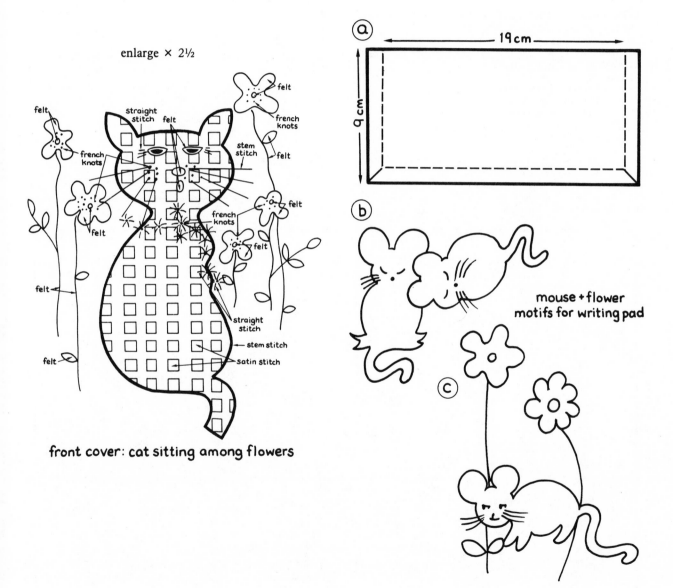

enlarge × 2½

felt

straight
stitch

felt

felt

french
knots

french
knots

felt

felt

french
knots

felt

felt

stem
stitch

felt

straight
stitch

stem stitch

satin stitch

front cover: cat sitting among flowers

ⓐ   19 cm

9 cm

ⓑ

mouse + flower
motifs for writing pad

ⓒ

FOR CHILDREN TO MAKE *(opposite)*

1 Collage Apron *(page 115)*
2 Teddy Bookmark *(page 117)*
3 Gingerbread Boy *(page 119)*
4 Mr Rainbow *(page 114)*
5 Felt Pencil Tops *(page 114)*
6 Teddy Bear Wall Hanging *(page 116)*
7 Christmas Tree Decoration *(page 113)*
8 Sweet Jar *(page 112)*
9 Toy Boat *(page 116)*
10 Lavender Trinket Box *(page 113)*
11 Draughts and Chess Set *(page 112)*
12 Shell Vase *(page 112)*
13 Felt Needlecases *(page 118)*

FOR THE CHRISTMAS TREE *(overleaf)*

1 Pressed Flower Miniatures *(page 125)*
2 Cotton Reel Man *(page 122)*
3 Flower Bookmarks, Prayer Bookmarks and Gift Tags *(page 131)*
4 Mobiles and Christmas Decorations *(page 123)*
5 Dancing Danny *(page 130)*
6 Crochet Lavender Hat *(page 123)*
7 Cotton Mould Figures *(page 120)*
8 Christmas Robin *(page 121)*
9 Mouse Bookmark *(page 127)*
10 Father Christmas Tree Decoration *(page 127)*
11 Bugs *(page 128)*
12 Hedgehog and Baby *(page 122)*
13 Bookworm Bookmark *(page 124)*
14 Hetty the Hallowe'en Witch *(page 126)*
15 Furry Fob Keyring *(page 120)*
16 Eggshell Decoration *(page 124)*

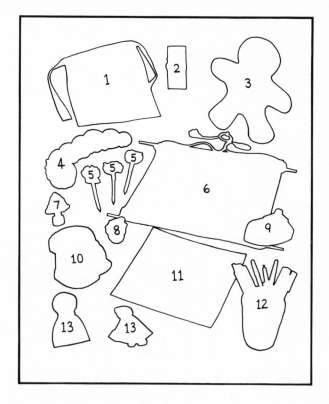

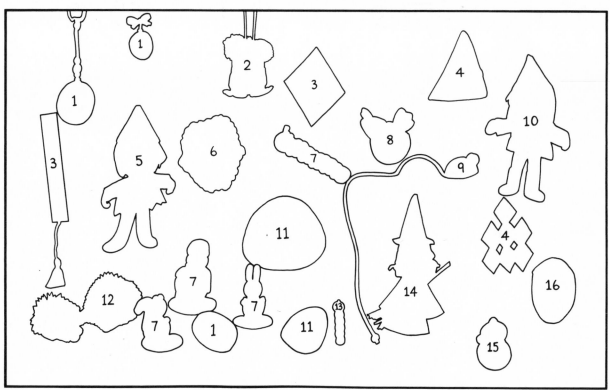

BAGS *(opposite)*
1 Picture Bag *(page 132)*
2 Needlepoint Purse *(page 133)*
3 Gift Bags *(page 133)*
4 Dolly Cocoon *(page 134)*
5 Playmat/Toybag *(page 135)*
6 Travel Handy *(page 138)*
7 Ooloo the Owl *(page 136)*

Book and Toy Holder
Jane Carter, Abingdon, Oxon

An extremely practical gift, this hessian holder will be an attractive feature in the bedroom or playroom and will encourage children to be tidy!

Materials
100×47cm and 100×27cm natural hessian
5m of 40mm wide cotton tape
scraps of material and felt for appliqué
wool embroidery thread, matching sewing thread
4 beads
iron-on Vilene
fabric glue
squared paper

Method
1 Divide smaller piece of hessian into four and mark with tailor's chalk or tacking thread.
2 Using squared paper size up the patterns for appliqué work and cut out each piece.
3 Choose suitable pieces of material for each figure and press carefully. Thin pieces may need strengthening with Vilene.
4 Pin paper patterns on back of material, draw round carefully, remove paper and cut out.
5 Place fabric pieces on the hessian so they are spaced evenly. They can be stuck with rubber solution or sewn round the edges with buttonhole stitch or machine stitch.
6 Make doll's hair from 9 pieces of wool 40cm long; leave 7cm in the middle of the wool, plait either end and tie off. Sew the middle on to the doll's face, stitching down the strands with matching thread. Tie embroidery thread bows on plaits. Embroider features in fine thread.
7 Make rocking horse's tail by winding wool round three fingers, cut one end of loop, tie other end with matching wool and sew on firmly. Sew on bead for eye or embroider with wool.
8 Sew on beads for teddy bear's nose and eyes. Cover nose bead with embroidery thread or wool by working from side to side, and then make a mouth.
9 Embroider edges of ball with feather stitch.
10 Complete book holder by pressing tape in half lengthways. Take the smaller piece of hessian and pin tape along top edge, so that the raw edge is right up to the folded edge of the tape. Pin, tack and stitch.
11 Pin this hessian to the larger hessian piece matching sides and bottom edges. Tack and stitch down sides and bottom seams. Stitch down pockets on marked lines taking care to double stitch at bound top as a reinforcement.
12 Starting at the bottom side edge, pin tape as before all round edges, folding under at corners to make neat mitres. Tack very carefully, then stitch on edge using either zig-zag or straight stitch.
13 To make hanging loops take 5 pieces of tape 12cm long. Fold over each end 5mm. Pin loops on tape at top of hanging, at equal distances. Tack and sew on carefully.
14 Put a piece of dowelling or cane through loops and hang on wall with cup-hooks.

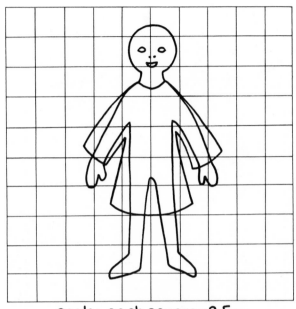

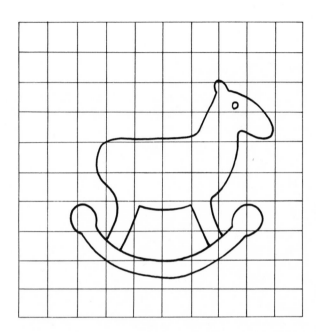

scale : each square = 2·5cm

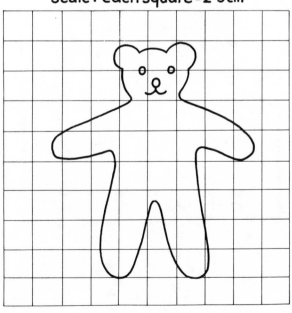

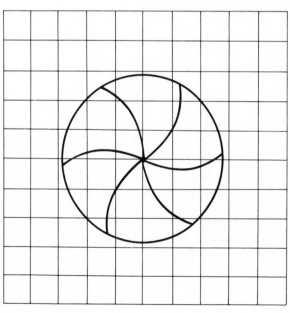

Potato-Print Apron

Jacki Galise, Ilford, Essex

A bright, easy-to-make, potato-printed apron using fabric printing inks on calico.

Materials
60 × 50cm white calico
red and green fabric printing inks
brush to apply dye
medium-sized potato
vegetable knife for cutting design
2.3m of 12mm red bias binding
2.7m of 12mm green straight binding tape
sewing cotton to match binding and fabric
newspapers

Method
1 Cut potato in half and cut out simple shape with tip of knife about 3mm deep.
2 Cut away parts you do not want to print (a).
3 Cut another part of design in remaining half of potato (b).
4 Blot off potato juice and apply printing ink.
5 Test your design on paper by pressing inked surface on newspaper pad.

To work design
1 Cut out fabric as shown (c) and mark out design as shown (d).
2 Lay fabric on several layers of newspaper. Print red flower heads then, when dry, print green stems and leaves (d). Fix dye in fabric by ironing or as described for your particular dye.
3 Cut out pockets and join (e). Sew binding to pocket and sew pocket to apron front.
4 Sew red and green binding on apron edges (f).

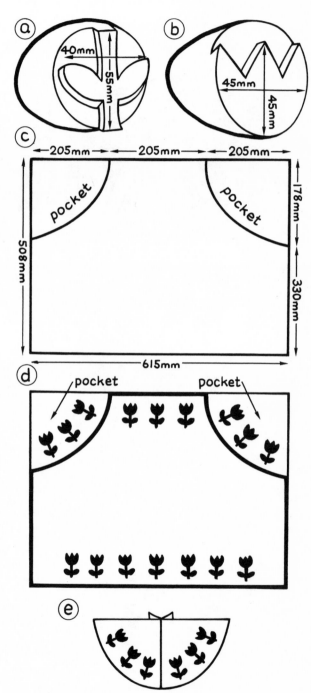

104

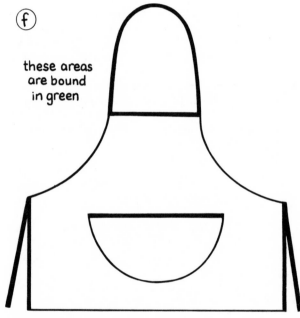

(f)

these areas are bound in green

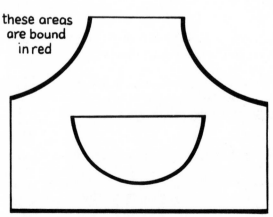

these areas are bound in red

Needlepoint Pincushion
Carole Biggin, Lincoln

A practical pincushion made from the lid of an aerosol spray and oddments of canvas, wool and fabric. You can work out your own design – simple, repeating geometrics work well.

Materials
straight-sided lid (from an aerosol spray)
single thread canvas (18 threads per inch)
stranded embroidery wool
sawdust to fill lid
small circle of fabric for top of pincushion
fabric adhesive
sewing and tacking thread
tapestry needle

Method
1 Measure depth of lid and add 2cm for turnings. Measure circumference of lid and add 1.5cm for joining canvas and ease allowance. Cut canvas to size.
2 Overlap short edges by 1cm, forming canvas into a cylinder. Align holes and secure by tacking together (a).
3 Turn over 1cm hem at both top and bottom, again aligning holes and securing with tacking thread (a). The prepared canvas should now drop over the plastic lid and be exactly the same depth but slightly more in circumference. A tight fit will be ensured when the wool is covering the wrong side as well as the design on the right side.
4 Using the lid to draw round, cut a circle of fabric 1.5cm larger all round than the lid. Notch edges (b).
5 Fill lid with sawdust, packing it down well.
6 Apply adhesive around top edge in a band approximately 1.5cm deep (c).
7 Place fabric over the top, firmly pressing on to the adhesive around edge. Leave to dry (c).
8 To work design on canvas, use double strands of

105

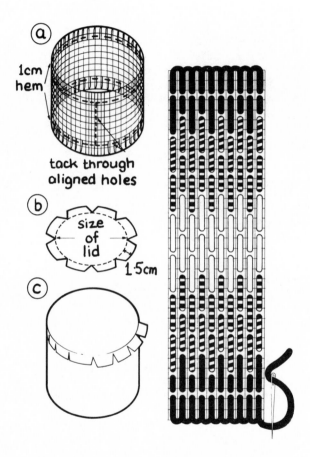

1cm
hem

tack through
aligned holes

size
of
lid

1·5cm

wool and neaten top and bottom edges with close buttonhole stitch worked through 2 threads of canvas mesh (d). Count the mesh to find the centre of the band. Work round centre, then up to the top and down to bottom, to ensure design is evenly balanced. The design shown is straight stitch, worked over 4 canvas threads. Count mesh around circumference to calculate whether the chosen design will join up evenly.

9   On completion of canvas embroidery, slip the canvas over the prepared lid from the top, then neatly stitch it with matching thread to edge of fabric. If desired the base of the lid may also be covered with fabric, as for the top.

Bath-Time Panda and His Cuddly Twin
Valerie Goodbury, Malvern, Worcs

Just the thing to encourage the reluctant washer, this puppet/flannel is designed to fit a child's hand; his twin can be filled with foam rubber to become a sponge.

Materials
20×90cm towelling, half black and half white (for 2 pandas)
matching thread
scrap of black felt
stranded embroidery cotton – white and black
stuffing – not kapok – or foam rubber

Method

1 With right sides together, join front legs to body C–D, and arms to front and back body pieces A–B.
2 Sew ears together in pairs, leaving open along bottom edge, turn right side out.
3 Pin body pieces together, pinning ears between the two layers (at this stage the ears will be pointing down, inside the body).
4 Pin back legs in place and stitch all round outer edge of body and legs.
5 *On puppet only* – overcast all raw edges.
6 Turn right side out.
7 Embroider eyes, on eye patches, using three strands of white cotton.
8 Taking care only to stitch the top layer of fabric, sew eye patches in place.
9 Using three strands of black cotton, embroider nose and mouth.
10 Gently stuff toy panda or cut panda shape out of 1in thick foam and ease into body. Stitch opening.

enlarge × 2

body front cut 1 white

body back cut 1 white

place to selvedge

back legs cut 1 black

front legs black cut 1 turn pattern over cut 1 more

arm black cut 2 turn pattern over cut 2 more

eye patch cut 2 black felt

ear black cut 2 turn pattern over cut 2 more

107

Sweet-Scented Pincushion

Diane Smith, Portsmouth

A dainty, sweet-smelling pincushion, too pretty to be hidden away in your sewing-box; 4.5cm high × 8cm wide.

Materials
23 × 18cm printed cotton
10 × 15cm foam 2cm thick
1 tablespoonful of potpourri
lid of 100g jar of coffee
50cm of lace trimming 2.5cm wide
small pins
glue

Method
1   Remove cardboard inner from coffee lid and retain.
2   Place lid on foam and use as guide to draw round. Cut out 2 circles of foam.
3   Put first circle of foam in lid, then put potpourri on top of this and second circle of foam on top of potpourri. Keep to one side ready for covering.
4   Place a saucer on a piece of printed cotton, draw round, then cut out. Run gathering thread round edge and place over foam and lid and pull up gathers tightly to fit under bottom of lid.
5   Use the cardboard inner from the coffee lid as a guide and draw round on piece of printed cotton. Cut out slightly larger. Place lid inner on fabric, draw the fabric round and glue, then glue this to bottom of coffee lid.
6   Sew short ends of lace together. Then gather inner edge of lace to fit tightly round top of pin cushion. Sew in place. Put a few pins in top of pin cushion for decoration.

Knitting Needle Case

Lætitia Stone, Plymouth

A convenient way of keeping your knitting needles – no more rummaging through an assorted bundle.

Materials
90 × 90cm medium-weight fabric – cotton, poly cotton, rayon
50 × 8cm Binca canvas or embroidery canvas
1.3m round elastic

Method
1   With right sides together join one long edge of inside holder A to one long edge of canvas. Stitch 1cm from edge, then neaten edges by zig-zag or overcasting, press turnings towards inside holder A and topstitch to hold them in place (a).
2   Repeat the process with the inside holder B and the other long edge of the canvas.
3   Dividing elastic in half, thread two rows through holes in canvas leaving 1–1.5cm space between rows. Begin and end with knot on wrong side of canvas and leave some slack between stitches (b). Allow for any extra large needles by making a few double-length stitches at one end. Be sure that the two rows of stitches match exactly.
4   Make top and bottom flaps by folding each in half lengthwise with right sides together; seam ends allowing 1cm turning. Turn right side out and press.
5   Match raw edges to long sides of inside holder, leave an equal space at each end, tack in place on right side (b).
6   Place inside and outside holder right sides together, allow 1cm turnings, seam around three sides leaving one short side open. Trim the corners and turn through to the right side and press. Press the flaps down towards the centre of the inside holder and top-stitch the outside edge to hold them down.
7   To make the bag, press down and tack a 1cm turning on wrong side of one of the 40cm sides of each piece.

8 Fold up neatened edge 14cm on right side of each piece to form bag and flap (c).

9 Place the two pieces together so that folded sides are together and right sides of flap are together. Make sure that inside folded edges match exactly (c).

10 Allowing 1cm turning, seam raw edges together, shaping flap as required. Trim and clip as necessary.

11 Through central open part of bag, turn through flap

and then one side of bag; the bag is now self-lined.

12 Insert raw edge of holder between outside and lining of bag, with outside of holder to outside of bag.

13 Machine across to attach holder to bag (d). Holder rolls up and tucks into bag.

14 A tie fastening can be made from remaining strip of fabric, or Velcro or a button fastening can be used to secure the flap.

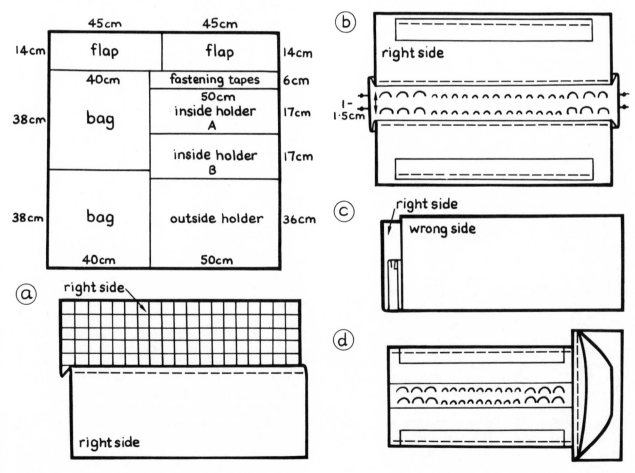

A Storytime Cushion

Sheila Scawen, Oadby, Leicester

This special cushion cover, with a pocket for a favourite story book, can be made to fit any small cushion or pillow. The illustrated cover was made to fit a cushion 26×31cm; patterned or picture fabric could be substituted for the hand-drawn picture.

Materials

50×50cm washable fabric
19×31cm white cotton
20×32.5cm polyester wadding
lace, ricrac or similar to edge cushion cover (optional)

Method

1 Quilted pocket. This should be the same width as the cushion and half to threequarters its depth. A smaller picture may be extended to the correct size by adding strips of material to the edges of the picture.
2 Using Finart Fabric Crayons draw a picture on paper (or let the recipient draw his or her own favourite picture).
3 Following the crayon manufacturer's instructions transfer the picture to the white fabric, and iron to fix the colours.
4 Sew on strips if these are needed to extend the picture.
5 Tack the picture to a piece of polyester wadding which is slightly larger than the picture. Using a fairly long machine stitch or hand-sewn running stitch, outline some of the bolder shapes in the picture to make them stand out from the background. Stitch, fairly closely, backwards and forwards across another section of the picture, eg the ground, or the sky, this will help to give depth to the picture.
7 Line the pocket by placing picture and lining right sides together and stitch across top edge only. If lace or other edging is being used, insert a piece in this seam.

8 Turn right sides out and tack pocket to cushion top. If using lace edging, tack the lace to cushion top so that lace lies towards centre.
9 Place cushion back and front right sides together, stitch round leaving a gap on one side, large enough to insert the cushion. Stitch the opening to close.

Miss Pinn

Ann Mary Johnstone, Aylesbury, Bucks

Miss Pinn not only looks attractive, she is extremely useful. Her mob cap is a pincushion, and additional pins are stored in the container under her skirt. Little Miss Pinn stands 10cm high; larger Miss Pinn 16cm high. Larger Miss Pinn is based on a container 5.5cm in diameter, 7.5cm high, a cotton reel body and 30mm ball for head. When deciding the size, choose items that give pleasing proportions.

Materials

small pot with press-on or screw top (ointment, cosmetic, handcream)
a cork about 4cm high
a hard cottonwool or polystyrene ball (about 20mm diameter) obtainable from craft shop
old tights, scraps of fine cotton, felt, lace or broderie anglaise
clear glue
synthetic stuffing

Method

1 Cover head ball with double layer of tights or make firmly stuffed ball of appropriate size. Stitch tightly below ball and wind cotton tightly round for 5mm to give small 'neck' (a).
2 Spread gathers out and stick surplus over the cork to cover 'body'. When dry, trim level with base of cork and stick body on lid of base container (b).
3 Cover the sides of the base container with fabric or felt using glue.
4 Cut strip of fabric slightly deeper than the container (allowing for width of 'hips') plus a tiny hem if edge

110

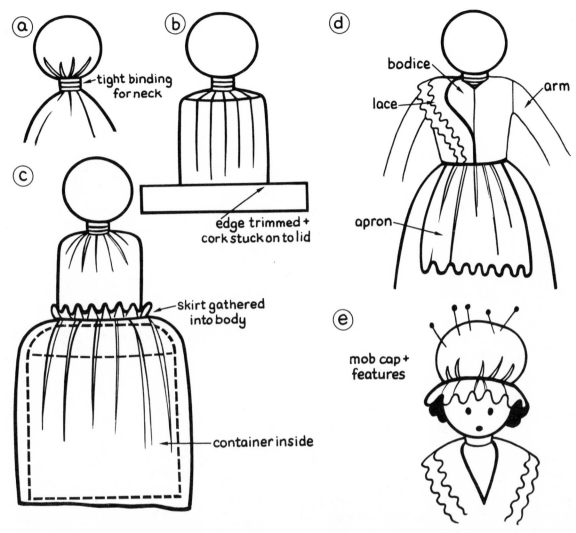

is not cut with pinking shears, and long enough to give a pleasing fullness. Join ends, hem if desired, gather, and attach round 'waist' (c).

5 Cut a strip of fabric to drape shawlwise over body, folding under at neck edge. Catch front edges together, trim off surplus round waist edge, allowing small turning. Catch bodice edge to waist, easing fullness where necessary.

6 Cut 2 strips of felt for arms, and stitch them to the bodice at shoulders (d).

7 Lay strip of narrow lace round shoulders to cover tops of arms, and stitch at waist. Gather piece of wide lace or broderie anglaise for apron and stitch in place (d).

8 Make a tiny flower with felt or embroidery cotton stems. Cut arm ends into simple hand shape, overlap hands and stitch the flower behind them.

9 For a mob cap pincushion, cut a circle of fabric about 10cm diameter, pink the edges and gather 10mm from the edge. Draw up to fit head, stuff and stitch in place, adding extra stuffing when almost attached, to give a firm cap (e). For a bonnet, cut a strip of fabric to go over head, allowing a good turning at front, and sufficient for fullness at back. Stitch on narrow lace at front, gather back and stitch in position.

10 Mark features with biro or felt-tip pen and put pins in cap (e).

111

FOR CHILDREN TO MAKE *illustrated in colour on page 97*

All these presents are simple and inexpensive – ideal gifts for children to make.

Draughts and Chess Set
Angela Collins (aged 12), Cullompton, Devon (from an idea by Anne Abraham)

Materials
26×26cm black card
24×24cm white card
26×26cm clear plastic covering
2×2×24cm wood
white and black paints
clear varnish
black felt-tip pen
paint brushes sizes 2, 8, 10
sandpaper
PVA glue

Method
1 Divide white card into 3cm squares (8 on each side) with black felt-tip pen.
2 Draw design in alternate squares to indicate 'black' squares.
3 Cover card with clear plastic covering.
4 Place white card on black card and mark 1cm surround. Glue back of white card and place card carefully in position on black card.

To make the draughts
5 Mark off wood into 1cm sections and cut into 24 pieces.
6 Smooth each piece of wood all over with sandpaper.
7 Using a No 8 brush, paint 12 pieces white and 12 pieces black.
8 Paint black patterns on white pieces and white patterns on black pieces.
9 When pieces are dry, cover with varnish.
10 To make chess pieces, use plastic wood moulded on top of squares before they are sandpapered and painted.

Shell Vase
Maria Dunster (aged 12), Cranbrook, Kent

Materials
Polyfilla
disposable container
plastic pot for vase
shells
varnish

Method
1 Mix 3tbsp Polyfilla with enough water to make stiff paste in disposable container.
2 Coat plastic pot with paste and arrange shells lengthwise around the pot. Leave to dry.
3 Apply two coats of varnish.

Sweet Jar
Tricia Reetham, Lings, Northampton

Materials
small glass jar
scrap of material
cardboard
ribbon
sweets
thread

Method
1 Cut out cardboard circle to fit top of jar.
2 Using pinking shears, cut out circle of material with a diameter 5cm larger than circle of card.
3 Stick card on wrong side of material, in central position.
4 Fill jar with small sweets.
5 Place the lid in position and secure with thread or an elastic band.
6 Trim as desired.

Lavender Trinket Box

Karma-Maria J. Putterill (aged 10), Llandysul, Dyfed

This little box can be used for jewellery, handkerchiefs or as a needle and cotton box – the needles being placed around the inside lining with the cottons on top of the cushion.

Materials

empty cheese-spread box
piece of card
oddments of material
glue
lavender

Method

1 Cover the two halves of the cheese box with material and glue down on wrong side.
2 Cut card to size to allow it to fit into the bottom half of the box in a cylinder. Using the card as a pattern, cut 2 pieces of material. Cover outside of card with one piece. Glue ends of card to make a cylinder, then stick cylinder firmly to half the cheese box.
3 Cut a circle of material using the box bottom as a pattern and stick to the inside bottom of the box to line it. Line the inside of the card with material already cut to size, tucking in edges to neaten, and glue.
4 Again using box bottom as pattern, cut 2 circles of material, sew round leaving small opening, turn to right side and stuff with lavender. Sew opening together and place in bottom of box. Add any small decorations as desired.

Christmas Tree Decoration

Lynne McCallum (aged 9), Boroughbridge, North Yorks

Materials

oddments of green, red and brown felt
beads
stuffing
white ricrac braid
thread

Method

1 Cut out pattern shapes and sew beads to both pieces of tree.
2 Put right sides of tree together and oversew edges leaving a space for the trunk.
3 Turn right side out and stuff lightly.
4 Oversew 3 sides of trunk and stuff lightly. Place trunk a little way inside tree and sew.
5 Oversew 3 sides of tub and stuff lightly. Place trunk a little way inside tub and sew. Sew ricrac braid round tub.
6 Make a loop with green thread and sew to top of tree.

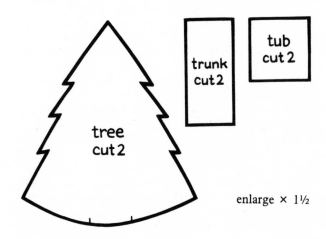

tree
cut 2

trunk
cut 2

tub
cut 2

enlarge × 1½

Mr Rainbow

Rebecca M. Boam, Newbold Verdon, Leics

Materials

6 10g balls of DK or 3-ply in different colours
oddment of wool for tail
2 15mm diameter plastic eyes
6 2cm diameter bells
small piece of red felt
glue
knitting needle
cardboard
scissors, compass, pencil, ruler

Method

1 To make templates for body pompons, draw 2 separate 27mm radius circles on cardboard, with smaller circles of 11mm radius inside them using same centre. Cut out the two rings.
2 Make 5 body pompons by first tying end of one of the coloured wools around the 2 cardboard templates, joining them together, and then continually winding it through centre and over top until entire circle is covered and centre hole filled.
3 Put knitting needle gently through the centre of circle and cut carefully through entire thickness of wool around rim of circle. Finally tie a 25cm length of wool tightly between templates and remove cardboard. Trim pompon where necessary in order to give a smooth ball.
4 Make tail in same way, using 18mm radius template with 9mm radius inner circle.
5 Make head in same way using 30mm radius template with 14mm radius inner circle.
6 Join pompons through middle using needle and length of wool, threading a bell between each pompon and then stick the pompons together firmly, leaving the bells free.
7 Stick on eyes, red nose and mouth from scrap of felt and two pieces of wool with thick knot at end for feelers.

Felt Pencil Tops

Kay Weeks, Dunstable, Beds

Daisy

Materials

6 × 3cm green felt
3cm diameter circle green felt
3cm diameter circle yellow felt
24 6cm lengths of white DK wool
pencil
glue
felt-tip pens
matching green sewing cotton

Method

1 Glue green strip round top of pencil.
2 Secure lengths of wool at centre with length of cotton, tying tightly.
3 Spread out and glue evenly on to yellow circle.
4 Place green circle on opposite side, stitch three-quarters of the way round.
5 Insert pencil with green strip into opening and continue stitching until firmly in place.
6 With felt-tip pens add face to yellow circle.

Peony

Materials

As for daisy but using 1.5m red wool instead of white

Method

1 As for daisy.
2 Wind wool 12 times round fingers, secure in centre with a length of cotton, tying tightly.
3 Continue as for daisy.

Dandy Lion

Materials

2 body shapes in orange felt as pattern (actual size)
2 3cm diameter circles in orange felt
2 small spots for eyes
24 6cm lengths of orange DK wool
pencil
glue
black felt-tip pen
orange sewing cotton

Method

1 Stitch body shapes together leaving base open. Glue pencil and insert into body.
2-5 As for daisy.
6 Glue on spots for eyes; with black felt-tip pen add nose and mouth.

yellow felt
scraps of different coloured felt
length of white ricrac braid
thread

Method

1 Hem round 3 sides of 28cm square of cotton.
2 Fold in 5mm all round long strip of cotton, then fold in half.
3 Place square inside fold in centre of strip, oversew edges and hem. Stitch square in place.
4 Cut 2 ducks from yellow felt as pattern.
5 Arrange pieces of blue and green felt along bottom of apron and sew in place.
6 Lay ducks to 'swim' on blue felt and sew on.
7 Attach ricrac braid along bottom of ducks. Cut out flower, stem and reed shapes and sew on to green felt.

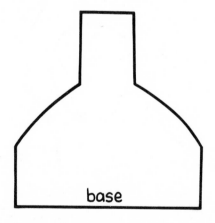

base

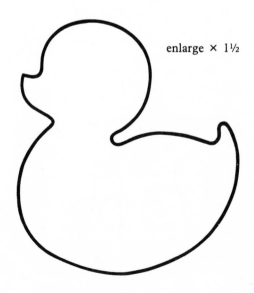

enlarge × 1½

Collage Apron

Lynne McCallum (aged 9), Boroughbridge, North Yorks

Materials

28 × 28cm cotton fabric
83 × 8cm cotton fabric

115

Toy Boat
Anne Malone, Barnet, Herts

Materials
polystyrene insulating board (available from DIY shops) or
   polystyrene packing
serrated kitchen knife
Copydex
section of eggbox, or cork, or narrow cotton reel
acrylic paints and brush

Method
1 Cut out polystyrene as pattern using a serrated
   kitchen knife. Keep knife upright and use gentle saw
   strokes. Do not force knife or you will tear
   polystyrene.
2 Cut funnel from centre of plastic eggbox. (A cork or
   thin cotton reel would do equally well.) Cut recess in
   deck for funnel. Glue pieces together with Copydex.
   Some glues dissolve polystyrene, so if you use any
   other glue it is advisable to try it out on an offcut
   first.
3 When glue is dry, paint boat using acrylic paints as
   these give added strength. The boat should have at
   least four coats of paint.

enlarge × 2

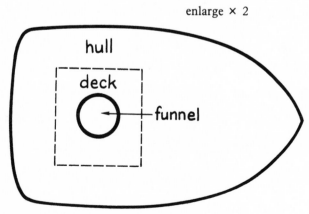

Teddy Bear Wall Hanging
Margaret King, Loughborough, Leics

Materials
45×60cm background fabric
30×30cm contrast fabric for picture
1 skein black stranded embroidery cotton
1m×6mm diameter thin dowelling
1.75m black cord
1m dowelling

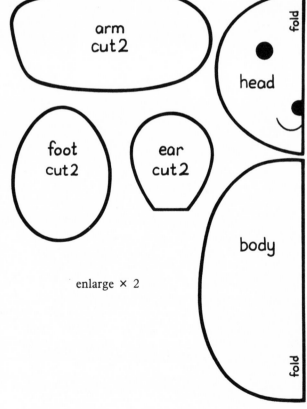

enlarge × 2

Method

1 Use pattern to cut out head, body, 2 arms, 2 feet and 2 ears from contrast fabric.
2 Pin bear centrally on fabric overlapping pieces.
3 Sew pieces on using blanket stitch.
4 Embroider eyes and nose in satin stitch and mouth in back stitch.
5 Fold under 2cm on either side of the background and stitch a double hem by hand or machine.
6 Fold under 2cm at top and bottom of background and stitch down leaving both ends open to form a channel.
7 Cut 2 pieces of dowelling 50cm long and insert 1 piece through the top channel and the other through the bottom leaving about 2.5cm protruding either side.
8 Fasten one end of cord to bottom left dowelling leaving 2.5cm hanging; run cord up to top left and knot, across top to right and knot, then down to bottom right and secure leaving 2.5cm hanging. Clovehitch knots may be used.
9 Fray the hanging ends of cord.

Teddy Bookmark
Victoria Skidmore (aged 13), Halesowen, West Midlands

Materials
15×6.5cm white card
fur fabric
ribbon
glue
black cotton
small scraps of felt
2 circles of card for eyes

Method

1 Trace and cut out the teddy pattern in fur.
2 Trace and cut out all felt pieces.
3 Sew on ears and paw pads.
4 Embroider paws in black cotton.
5 Glue on eyes and colour in pupils.
6 Tie a ribbon in a bow around teddy's neck.
7 Glue teddy on card.
8 Add trimmings of red ribbon on top and bottom of card.

enlarge × 1½

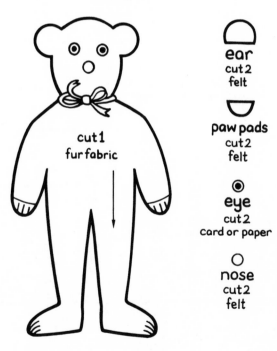

ear
cut 2
felt

paw pads
cut 2
felt

eye
cut 2
card or paper

nose
cut 2
felt

cut 1
fur fabric

Felt Needlecases

Dorothy Luce, St Lawrence, Jersey

Materials

pieces of red, black, peach and orange felt, plus scraps in other
  colours
fabric for lining (trim with pinking shears to prevent fraying)
fine gold braid
scrap of lace
embroidery cottons

Method

1   To make soldier, cut out red felt for tunic, and cut
    out 2 or 4 lining pieces slightly smaller.
2   Place lining between red felt, place face on top and
    stitch through all layers at neck.
3   Sew round hat leaving bottom edges open, insert face
    and top of tunic into opening, and sew together at
    bottom of hat.
4   Over neck stitching, stitch black collar and lace trim;
    stitch trim down front of tunic and black felt eyes,
    and embroider red mouth.
5   To make little girl, cut out cape, and cut out 2 or 4
    lining pieces slightly smaller.
6   Place lining between cape pieces and place lace trim
    between front edges of hood. Stitch through all
    layers round edge of hood.
7   Cut out and stitch arm in place, stitching hand at
    lower end.
8   Make tiny flowers from felt, stitch in place and stitch
    stems in embroidery cotton under hand.

enlarge × 1½

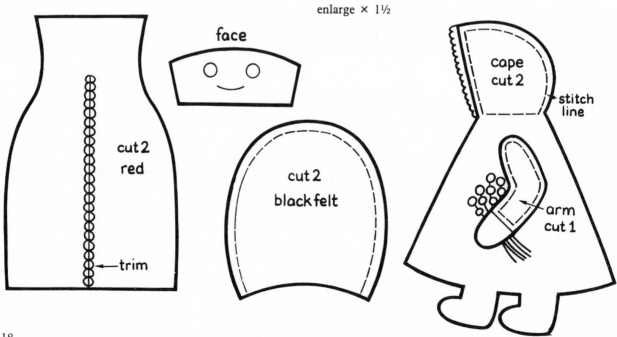

118

Gingerbread Boy

Margaret Webb, Hitchin, Herts

Materials

50cm fur fabric
5 black safety buttons
black felt for mouth
1m braid for icing
stuffing

Method

1 Cut pieces as pattern.
2 Attach eyes and buttons to front.
3 Right sides facing, sew pieces together leaving a gap for turning.
4 Turn right side out, stuff and sew up opening with ladder stitch.
5 Glue on braid.
6 Add felt for mouth.

enlarge × 2½

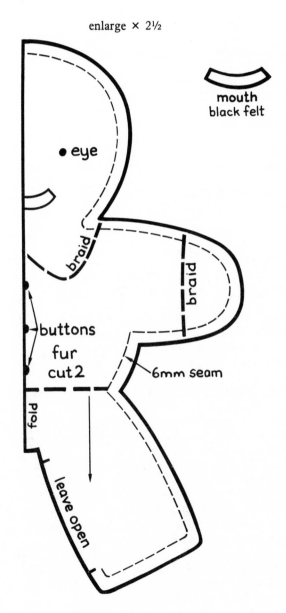

119

FOR THE CHRISTMAS TREE *illustrated in colour on pages 98 and 99*

A selection of small presents and decorations that might be suitable to hang on a Christmas tree or to decorate the table on special occasions such as Easter or Hallowe'en.

Cotton Mould Figures
Patricia Keen, West Drayton, Middlesex

Materials
cotton moulds, cotton beads or wooden beads in assorted sizes and colours
pipe cleaners or chenille stems and bump chenille in assorted colours
scraps of cardboard, felt, guipure lace daisies and beads
old scissors
felt-tip pen
PVA or rubber adhesive

Snowman
1 Cut 2 circles 4.5cm in diameter in thin card and 1 in white felt. Stick card circles together and felt circle on top.
2 Take large white cotton mould and stick half of a 2cm strip of chenille in hole. Stick remainder of chenille strip inside small white mould so that head and body touch. Stick snowman on to base and leave to dry.
3 Cut 4cm strip of black chenille and bend one end to form walking stick.
4 Cut 2 1cm strips of white chenille and stick on each side of snowman for arms. Glue walking stick to one arm and to base.
5 Cut 11cm strip of brightly coloured chenille, wind it around snowman's neck and stick in place. Wind 9cm strip of black chenille around tip of one finger and stick to snowman's head for hat.
6 Give snowman 2 small beads for eyes, 1 for nose and 3 for buttons, and glue in place.

Caterpillar
1 Stick 5 multi-coloured cotton moulds together with another larger mould for head.

2 Make 2 dents in head (except when using wooden beads) and stick on 2 1cm strips of green chenille for antennae.
3 Cut 5 4cm strips of green chenille and bend each into 'U' shape. Stick each 'U' shape upside down in gap where moulds have been stuck together.
4 Mark 2 eyes and nose with felt-tip pen.

Rabbit and Squirrel
1 For each animal cut 2 circles 3.5cm in diameter in card and 1 in felt. Stick card circles together and felt circle on top.
2 Take medium and small moulds and stick them together with 2cm piece of chenille as for snowman. Stick body to base.
3 For feet cut 1cm piece of chenille, fold it in half and stick to base.
4 For each arm cut 1cm strip of chenille and stick one on each side of body.
5 Draw face with felt-tip pen, and stick flowers to base.
6 Rabbit. Cut 10mm strip of chenille and stick on for tail; cut 2 15mm strips of chenille and stick into dents on top of head for ears.
7 Squirrel. Cut 2 5mm strips of chenille and stick on head for ears. Cut 1 chenille 'bump' and bend into 'S' shape, stick tail to back of animal and to base.

Furry Fob Key Ring
Alison Riley, Burbage, Leics

Materials
scraps of fur fabric
stuffing
1 key ring fitment
several small beads
1 pair of 5mm goo-goo eyes
clear adhesive

Method
1 Body. Cut 6cm diameter circle of fur, run gathering thread around edge. Stuff firmly and fasten off.

2 Head. Cut 5cm diameter circle of fur and prepare as for body. Sew head to body.

3 Thread a few beads onto length of strong thread and tie around neck.

4 Stitch two beads to body as buttons.

5 Glue eyes into position.

6 Sew key ring fitment to top of head using strong thread.

Christmas Robin

Rosemary Pritchard, Bristol

Materials

card for template
cotton wool or kapok for stuffing
scraps of felt in brown, red, white, yellow and black
sewing thread
cord for hanging

Method

1 Make pentagon template, then cut out all pattern pieces as indicated (size as illustrated).

2 Body. Oversew 6 brown pentagons together; pentagons are first joined to each side of central one, and outer pentagons are then joined together (a).

3 Oversew remaining 6 pentagons together as indicated (b).

4 Join these two pieces (c) together to make a ball shape, leaving 2 sides open. Turn right side out and stuff. Close the opening neatly.

5 Wings. Oversew together in pairs, using double running stitch along dotted lines. Sew firmly on to robin as shown (a).

6 Tail. Oversew together, then use double running stitch along dotted lines. Sew firmly on to robin as shown (a).

7 Beak. Fold in half and sew in position (b).

8 Eyes. Either use small black beads or cut 2 circles of black felt. Run a gathering thread around the edge, pull up and fasten tightly. Sew in position (b).

9 To finish, fix on cord for hanging at point X (a).

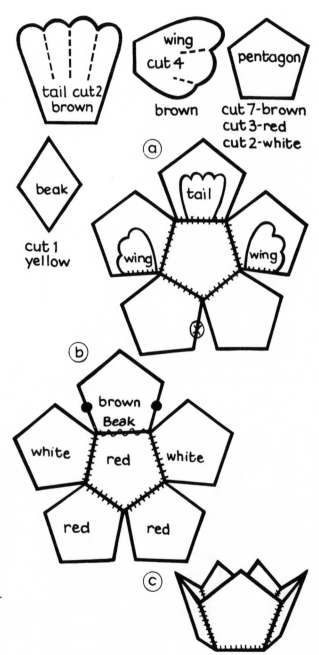

121

Cotton Reel Man
Averil Furness, Norwich

Materials
cotton reels (or pieces of broom handle 3cm long)
paint
scraps of fur or fur fabric
round bead elastic
scraps of felt
thin card
glue

Method
1 Paint cotton reels with pink paint (small tins of non-toxic paint sold for model kits are quick-drying and safe for children). Two or three coats of paint may be needed.
2 Mark on features with paint, crayons or felt pens (a). Using red crayon smudge circle on each side of face for cheeks.
3 Cut circle of fur slightly larger than top of cotton reel. Using piece of elastic 15cm long, thread each end separately through piece of fur from right side and knot on wrong side. Glue fur to top of cotton reel for hair.
4 Trace feet and hand shapes on to thin card. Using these as templates, cut hands and feet from brightly coloured pieces of felt. Glue in position. It may be necessary to weight the bottom of each cotton reel with plasticine before gluing on the feet to counter-balance the hair. (Size of feet and hands as illustrated.)
5 Variations can be made using different brightly coloured paints and by decorating in different ways, eg add a cone of felt as a hat to make a clown. Several little men can be made into a mobile for a child's bedroom, suspended at different heights on fine elastic.

Hedgehog and Baby
Priscilla S. Douglas-Jones, Glyndyfrdwy, Corwen

Materials
1 large teazel
1 small teazel
small pieces of black felt
6 pins
1 tbsp Polyfilla, or use flour mixed with a few drops of Dettol
black enamel paint

Method
1 Cut off stalk and any long spines at back of large teazel.
2 Cut spines flat on one side to make base.

122

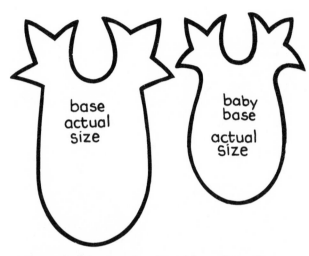

base
actual
size

baby
base
actual
size

Method
1 Cut out shapes in different colours (size as shown).
2 Glue shapes together by the points; many different patterns can be made from these 3 basic shapes.
3 Add sequins and thread for hanging.

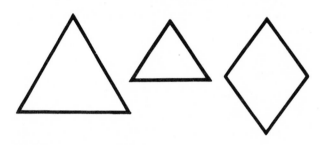

3 Trim back spines for about 10mm from tip.
4 Cut base from black felt as pattern.
5 Stick felt on to base with paws sticking out on either side of trimmed end. Trim off any surplus on back and sides.
6 Mix Polyfilla with a little water. Make small balls and press on to pin heads. Stick pins into piece of Oasis or cork and allow to dry.
7 Turn Oasis upside down, dip balls into black paint, and allow to dry.
8 Push one pin into teazel for nose and two close against prickles and rather low down for eyes.
9 Baby. Make in same way but using smaller pattern for felt and smaller balls for eyes and nose.

Mobiles and Christmas Decorations
Kay Weeks, Dunstable, Beds

Materials
scraps of felt
sequins
glue
cotton or tinsel thread

Crochet Lavender Hat
Eileen Jennings, Bristol

Materials
No 20 crochet cotton
1.25 crochet hook
lavender

Method
Round 1: 2ch, 12dc into 1st ch from hook
Round 2: 2dc into each dc
Round 3: 1dc into 1st dc * 2dc into next dc, 1 dc into next dc, repeat from * to end of round
Rounds 4–8: 1dc into each dc
Round 9: working into back of the loop only, work 2dc into each dc
Rounds 10–12: 1dc into each dc
Round 13: 3ch for 1st tr, 1tr into each dc, ss into top of 3ch
Round 14: 1ch, 1dc into 1st ch space, * 2tr into next ch space, 2dc into next ch space, repeat from * to next ch space. Fasten off.
Base. Work rounds 1–5. Fasten off.
Finish off by filling crown of hat with lavender. Sew base to cover. Add trimming to hat.

Bookworm Bookmark

Alison Riley, Burbage, Leics

Materials

piece of narrow leather thong
5 pony beads 8mm in diameter
1 wooden bead for head 1cm in diameter
1 pair of 5mm goo-goo eyes
clear adhesive

Method

1   Cut 30cm off the piece of leather thong. Coat 4cm of one end of the thong in glue.
2   Thread the 5 pony beads on this glued end in turn, applying the glue between each bead with a cocktail stick, so that all the beads are glued together and firmly stuck to the thong.
3   In the same way, glue the wooden bead to the top of the thong for the head, leaving about 3mm of thong showing.
4   Glue the eyes to the head as shown, using a small drop of glue applied with a cocktail stick.
5   Wipe away any glue that is showing with a cocktail stick dipped in acetone.
6   To mark your page, just put the bookworm's tail inside the book and leave him peeping out at the top.

Eggshell Decoration

Diana J. Brown, Haddington, E. Lothian

Materials

blown egg
small hacksaw blade
thick gold thread
velvet ribbon
sequins, same colour as ribbon
Christmas cake decoration, eg bell
glitter
glue

Method

1   Mark cutting lines on egg with pencil (a). Using hacksaw, carefully cut along lines, smooth edges with sandpaper, and wash and dry shell.
2   Decorate shell outside with sequins, gold thread, etc, using glue (b), making hanging loop from thread at top. Stick glitter to inside of shell and hang a tiny decoration inside from top (c).

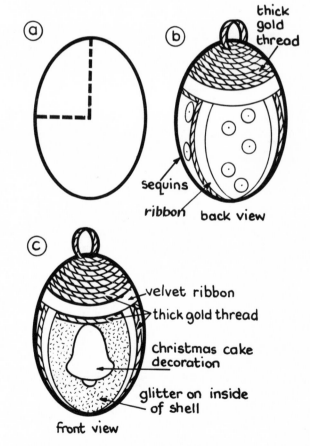

Pressed Flower Miniatures
Angela Aston, Wednesbury, West Midlands

The technique of pressing flowers is well known and many good definitive books are available from local libraries and bookshops. The beauty of many pressed flower pictures lies not only in the colours but also in the shape and delicacy of the finished work. Miniature pictures have an appeal of their own and care must be taken to preserve the fragile beauty of the minute flowers. Many flowers may lose their natural colour when pressed or the tone may vary as the moisture dries out of the petals, but the art of producing a good picture lies in mixing the *pressed* colours and also in creating an attractive design. It is often best to keep designs simple and not use too many colours or the finished result may look more like confetti.

Pressed flower miniatures may seem a little forbidding at first but they are always worth the effort involved. There are several advantages in pressing small flowers and florets, for example:

(i) a little goes a long way – one head of a flower such as alyssum will break down into literally hundreds of tiny single florets;

(ii) parts of flowers can be used such as stamens – these can be taken from faded blooms before throwing them away; daffodils, tulips, rhododendrons, lilies, freesias and even gladioli provide a wealth of colours, all of which can be put to imaginative use;

(iii) the smaller the flower the more versatile it is. A child's small flower press, about 15cm square, is more than adequate for the size of flowers being pressed.

Technique
There are several watchpoints which must be considered when pressing small flowers.

1 Many small flowers are florets snipped from a larger bloom eg lilac, hydrangea, alyssum, best done with the aid of a pair of sharp pointed scissors – the type used for embroidery are ideal.

2 Small flowers are by their nature far more fragile than their larger cousins and careful handling is needed if they are not to fall apart when being lifted. A large darning needle is useful for loosening the flower prior to picking it up and a pair of small tweezers come in handy.

3 Gluing can be tricky. If too much glue is used there is a risk that the colour will be leached out by the solvent base of the adhesive. Water-based glues such as Gloy or School glue are the easiest to use as a very small amount can be picked up on the end of a matchstick or cocktail stick and this can then be touched to strategic points of the flower before placing it in position. It is often only necessary to glue the centre of the flower but occasionally it may be necessary to glue the tips of petals or leaves to maintain their positions for mounting purposes. (Acetate frame covers hold a lot of static electricity and will attract unglued petals when placing them over the finished picture, resulting in crumpled flowers – the only solution is to glue down as much as possible.)

4 Glue on paper backgrounds where possible. If using fabric, first glue this to stiff paper or thin card; this will help to eliminate bubbles and creases in the background.

5 'Blank' boxes, key ring fobs, brooches, pendants, etc, to hold pressed flower arrangements can be obtained from craft shops.

Flower Collecting
Perhaps the most exciting part of creating miniatures is in collecting the flowers. It is amazing how much detail nature puts into her flowers and their full glory can only be appreciated by getting down to ground level.

A good imagination helps in making good use of what you find. The blossom on trees and shrubs can be effectively used as well as garden flowers. Tiny sprays of buds such as the tips of forget-me-not stems are useful as well as the complete flowers pressed flat.

Hetty the Hallowe'en Witch

Sheena C. Booth, Rayleigh, Essex

Materials

23cm square of black felt (sufficient for 3 witches)
23mm wooden or cotton ball for head
scraps of 4 ply wool for hair
flesh-coloured poster paint
cocktail stick or matchstick
round lollipop stick or twig 7cm long
dried grass or thin twigs
clear adhesive (UHU or Bostick)

Method

1 Cut one of each pattern piece from black felt (size as shown).
2 Glue down side of body A–C and overlap B–D, matching A–B and C–D to make a cone.
3 Glue neck edge and front edges of cape as shown on pattern. Stick in place on body cone with join of body at back.
4 Push matchstick partly into hole in ball. Paint ball and when dry stick to top of body, inserting remainder of matchstick through hole in top of cone.

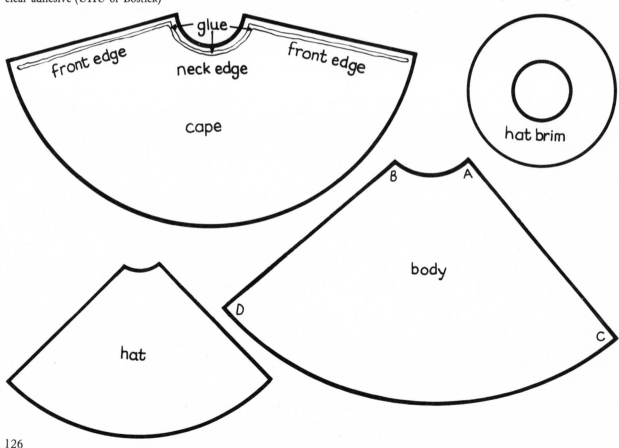

5 To make hair, wind wool 20 times around three
   fingers. Tie hank and slide off fingers. Cut loops.
   Stick tied centre to top of head and arrange hair
   round head, sticking if necessary.
6 Glue hat brim to top of head. Make top of hat as for
   body and glue in place on top of head.
7 Mark features with felt-tip pen.
8 Tie small twigs or grass round 7cm stick to make
   broom. Glue in place across front of body.
9 Sew a loop of black thread to top of hat to hang doll.

Mouse Bookmark
Celia Birch, Epsom, Surrey

Materials
small piece of coloured felt
small amount of soft stuffing
100cm 2-ply wool for tail
2 small glass beads for eyes
black cotton for nose and whiskers

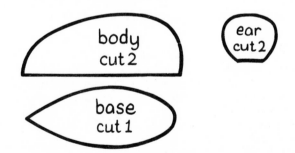

Method
1 Sew body pieces and base together, leaving opening
   at side of base for stuffing (size as shown).
2 Stuff and push into shape, sew opening.
3 Sew on ears and eyes.
4 Make nose with oversewing stitches. Knot some
   lengths of cotton for whiskers.
5 Plait tail and sew to base of body.

Father Christmas Tree Decoration
Andrea Peters, Hollywood, Birmingham

Materials
12×12cm red felt
5×8cm black felt
scraps of pink felt
pipe cleaner
glue fabric
10×10cm card
small piece of glitter thread
white DK wool
cotton wool
wooden or cotton wool ball 3cm diameter

Method
1 Cut out pattern pieces (size as shown).
2 Place jacket back right side down and stick hands in
   position. Place trousers with small amount of glue on
   jacket back.
3 Cut pipe cleaner 9cm long and bend in middle. Place
   in position shown on diagram.
4 Spread wrong side of front jacket with adhesive and
   stick to back of jacket.
5 Spread adhesive on one pair of boots and stick to
   trouser legs, then place other pair of boots on top.

127

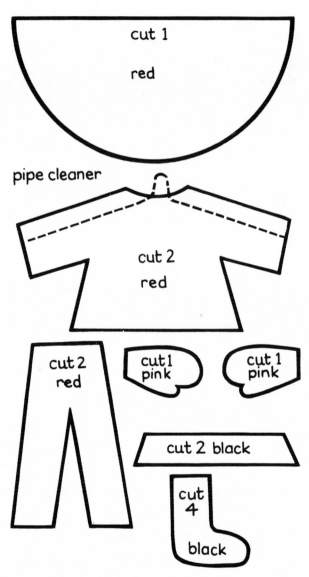

6 Cut 2 belts and stick in position on front and back of jacket.
7 Push protruding pipe cleaner into hole drilled in wooden ball or pressed cotton wool ball and secure with glue.
8 To make hair, cut piece of card 10cm deep and wind white/cream DK wool around 15 times. Carefully slide loops off card and secure with wool in centre. Cut loop ends.
9 Spread hair area with glue and stick down hair, tied centre at crown of head. Trim ends round face neatly.
10 Using felt-tip pen mark two eyes.
11 Form hat into cone sticking straight edges together. Spread glue round rim of hat and stick to hair.
12 Using small amount of cotton wool as beard, attach to chin.
13 Make a loop with glitter thread and thread through top of hat.

Bugs
Wendy Hawkin, Rickmansworth, Herts

Materials
10 × 17cm white felt for single bug
12 × 27cm white felt for bug family (mother and two babies)
fabric dye (Printex diluted with water, Dylon cold water dyes mixed up strongly with 'fix' added, or diluted fabric paints can be used)
perle sewing thread
beads for eyes
'flower stamen' or fuse wire for feelers
stuffing
cartridge paper
glue
spray diffuser (obtainable cheaply from any artists' supply shop) or use a toothbrush and pencil

Method
1 Fix felt to vertical surface, eg wall or board, with masking tape or Blu-tack.

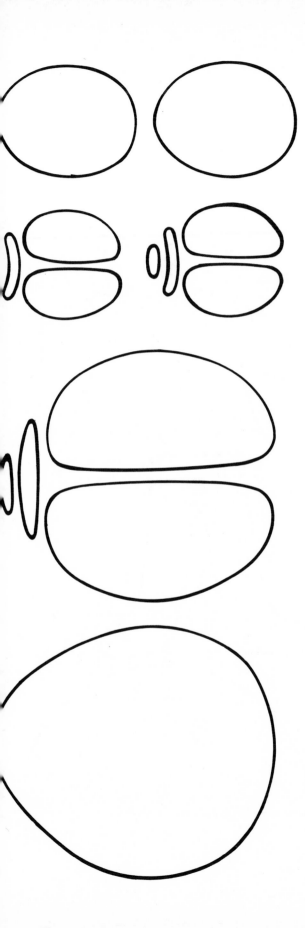

2 Trace pattern on to cartridge paper and cut the holes out (these are to spray through). Size can vary.

3 Place the mask centrally over felt and fix in place – Blu-tack is useful here.

4 Spray with fabric dyes. Red and blue are used here for the single bug, blue and green with a touch of purple for the family of bugs.

5 Allow to dry. Press with a warm iron.

6 Cut round shapes leaving a margin of 5mm (less for baby bugs).

7 The feelers are made from artificial flower stamens, which can be painted. Fuse wire curled at the ends can be used instead (a). Bend stamens round and fix inside top piece of felt with a dab of glue (b).

8 Starting at tail, sew top and bottom together with perle or other decorative thread, using buttonhole stitch. Leave 3cm open for stuffing.

9 Stuff until fairly well padded and complete sewing.

10 Sew two beads in place for eyes.

To make ladybirds, spray in red and print the spots before sewing by dipping the end of a round pencil in black fabric dye and pressing it on the felt where the spots are needed.

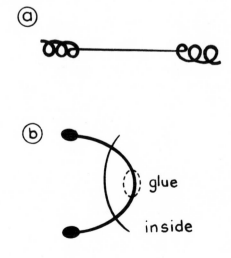

Dancing Danny

Kay Weeks, Dunstable, Beds

Materials

óddments of red and green felt
195cm brown DK wool
1 table-tennis ball
1 pipe cleaner
20cm long wooden houseplant stake
length of shirring elastic
glue
black felt-tip pen

Method

1 Glue leg shapes together. All pieces actual size.
2 Glue leg shapes to base of back body shape.
3 Make 2 holes in table-tennis ball, 1 for neck, 1 at top of head.
4 Fold pipe cleaner in half, attach shirring elastic to bend and push this through the ball leaving 2cm protruding at top of head.
5 To shape arms, bend pipe cleaner and glue just inside top of back body shape; fold over 1cm to form hands.
6 Glue on front body shape and add felt circles as buttons.
7 Arrange and glue wool to top of ball as hair.
8 Glue hat shape along straight edge, place on hair around shirring elastic with join down back.
9 Draw on face with felt-tip pen.
10 Attach end of shirring elastic to houseplant stake.

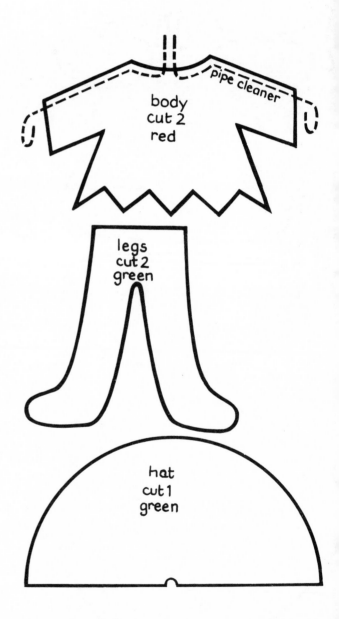

Pressed Flower Bookmarks, Prayer Bookmarks and Gift Tags

Carol S. Barnes, Faversham, Kent

Materials

coloured card of medium thickness
clear Fablon
oddment of wool
crochet hook of medium size
needle for sewing wool
Copydex glue
cocktail stick
scissors
tweezers
craft knife
metal ruler
hole punch
pressed flowers, green fern, leaves
embroidery silk

Bookmark

Method

1 Mark out and cut card 3.5 × 17cm with craft knife, using a metal ruler as a guide. Use cutting board underneath.
2 Choose small pressed flowers to tone or contrast with colour of card and arrange in place using tweezers. Start with smallest at top, getting larger towards bottom, but leave 2cm free at bottom for punch hole. When all flowers are in position pick up each one in turn, put very small dab of glue on back with cocktail stick and place in position. Then arrange and glue very small pieces of leaf or fern in between each flower, at an angle pointing upwards or whatever looks attractive. When complete, make sure there is no excess glue or dust remaining.
3 Remove protective backing from Fablon and place Fablon sticky-side-up on the table. Carefully lower bookmark flower-side down on to Fablon and press on. Turn bookmark over and smooth Fablon all round and in between flowers and to edges evenly, starting in middle. Turn over face-down again and trim off excess Fablon with craft knife close to edges.
4 Punch hole centrally at bottom of bookmark (centre of hole about 12mm from bottom edge).
5 To make tassel, make 20 chain length with crochet hook and wool. Fasten off, leaving about 15cm wool at beginning of chain and about 18cm of wool at the end of chain.
6 Wind wool round 4 fingers 12 times. Remove from fingers, hold in middle and tie in a bunch, centrally, with 18cm-length end of chain close to last chain stitch. Fold the two sides of the bunch together and wind the 18cm piece of wool tightly round the tassel about 1cm from the chain. Fasten off neatly with needle. Hold tassel ends together and trim straight with scissors.
7 Now thread 15cm end of wool with needle, pass through punch hole in bookmark and fasten off neatly by sewing into chain at the bottom of bookmark.

Prayer Bookmark

A small bookmark for prayerbooks can be made in exactly the same way as above by using 1.75 × 10cm size card with toning embroidery silk for tassel – using it 6 strands thick. Wind round fingers only 9 times, but crochet 20 chain using a slightly smaller crochet hook. Also use a smaller punch hole.

Gift Tag

1 Cut card 5 × 5cm. Glue two or three flowers with or without fern according to space.
2 Finish off with Fablon in the same way as for a bookmark, using a small punch hole in top corner about 7mm from edge.
3 Cut a 20cm length of toning embroidery silk, fold in half and knot ends together. Thread through punch hole passing knotted end through loop. Pull tight.

BAGS *illustrated in colour on page 100*

Picture Bag

Jen Harris, Coventry

An easy-to-make fabric bag with a modern, individual look. The bag itself – 40cm wide and 30cm deep – is quite spacious and would be suitable for shopping, school or the beach.

Materials

0.5m blue denim or similar fabric
0.5m lining fabric
iron-on interfacing
oddments of different fabrics

Method

1 Cut out all pieces of bag and bag lining (a). 6mm seams have been allowed on patterns.
2 Draw a rectangle 37 × 29cm on a piece of paper. Round off two corners. Divide rectangle into sixteen squares and draw in houses etc using squares as a guide (b).

3 Trace off all basic shapes of picture on to iron-on interfacing, adhesive side up if applicable. The blue denim forms the sky. Windows can be traced on to interfacing in the usual way or a piece can be cut out of the main building piece and fabric placed under this when you assemble the whole picture.
4 Select suitable fabrics for buildings etc, bearing in mind that you need not always use the right side, and that materials that fray a lot may be difficult to work with. Iron interfacing pieces on to wrong side of selected materials. Cut them out.
5 You will now have a variety of pieces that fit together like a jig-saw puzzle. Pin them in place on the right side of one main bag piece.
6 When all materials are in place including all doors and windows, set sewing machine to zig-zag stitch width 4, length ½. This will produce satin stitch. Sew all round edges of pinned pieces, using different coloured cottons as you wish. The bag front is now complete.

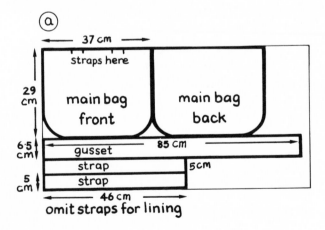

132

7 With wrong sides together, pin gusset to bag front, easing round corners. Sew, taking 6mm seam. Sew gusset to bag back in the same way.

Fold both straps lengthwise with the edges tucked-in. They should be 20mm wide. Sew along fold. Attach a strap to bag front where shown, with the fold inside. Repeat for back. Pin straps edge to edge with bag, so that they hang down at this stage.

8 Assemble lining pieces as you did for denim. With right sides together, place denim bag inside lining. Pin and sew together round top of bag, leaving space for turning at the back. Turn to right side. Fold in remaining edge and top stitch all round top of bag.

Gift Bags
Pat Myers, Bristol

Instead of spending money on expensive wrappings for gifts which are nearly always discarded, why not make it a double gift by making personalized gift bags? The bags are ideal for packing things in to go on holiday, or on the beach to hold watches, jewellery, loose change, etc, or they can be hung on the tree at Christmas. Make fancy ones for ladies, plain ones for men, delicate ones for babies – the choice is endless. The bags shown are 18×15cm finished size but these measurements can be altered to suit requirements.

Materials
2 pieces 19×24cm chosen fabric
1.1m cord
embroidery silks

Method
1 Cut 2 pieces of material 19×24cm.
2 On the right side of one piece embroider initials, flowers, etc. Either use manufactured transfers or trace pictures and transfer with an embroidery pencil. Press completed design on the wrong side.

3 With right sides together join bottom seam and side seams to within 6cm of top.
4 Neaten remaining part of side seam singly.
5 Turn top hem of bag over on to wrong side, to form a deep hem, and stitch twice, leaving enough room between rows of stitches, to thread cord.
6 Thread a double row of cord through the hem and draw up.

Needlepoint Purse
Julia D. Simkin, Birmingham

A neat purse which can be made to any design or shape. This one measures 10×14cm. If you design your own motif with the recipient's name or initials the present will become that much more special.

Materials
4 skeins of tapestry wool
piece of tapestry canvas of required size
remnant of velvet for backing
tapestry needle
graph paper

Method
1 Draw out a design on graph paper.
2 Using one hole of the canvas per square, begin stitching the pattern by tramming.
3 When complete, sew finished tapestry to velvet (velvet stops the purse from slipping against clothes when worn). Turn right-side-out.
4 Using left-over wool, cut into lengths long enough to go over the shoulder or round the neck.
5 Using several strands, divide into three and plait. Stitch to the sides of the bag.
6 The plait should be knotted at both ends and a tassel left to give a finished effect.
7 Press studs can be added if required.

Dolly Cocoon
Carol S. Barnes, Faversham, Kent

No little mother should be without one! This cocoon for dolls can also double as a papoose carrier if the child puts her arms through the handles.

Materials
30×85cm plain quilted fabric
35×21cm plain quilted fabric
30×85cm patterned or toning check lining
1m broderie anglaise or nylon lace

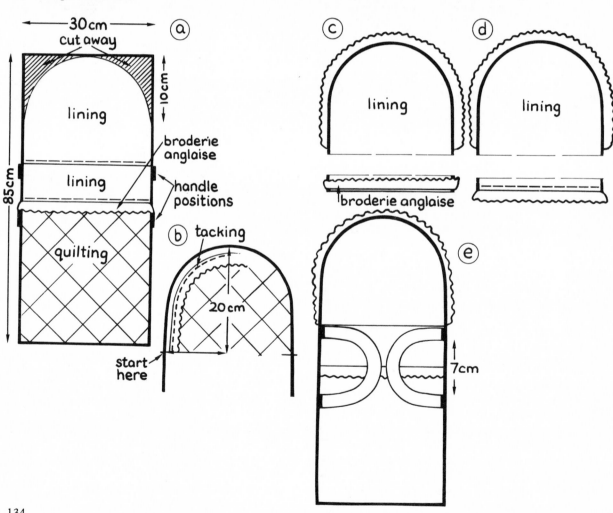

Method

1 Take 30×85cm piece of quilted fabric and lining. Place right sides together. Pin on the pattern for the shaped top of the cocoon and cut the quilted fabric and the lining together (a).

2 Pin and then tack the broderie anglaise around the curve starting about 20cm from top (b), placing the bias edge of the broderie anglaise to the edge of the right side of the quilting, facing inwards. Keep the tacking close to the bias edge of the broderie anglaise.

3 Pin and then tack the lining on to the quilting, right sides together, sandwiching the broderie anglaise between, and continuing down the long sides of the cocoon about 1cm from the edge (tack on the existing tacking stitches around the curve). Machine stitch all round tacking, taking great care around the curve. Turn right side out and press carefully, avoiding squashing the gathered broderie anglaise.

4 Pin and tack a strip of broderie anglaise to the bottom, right side of broderie anglaise to lining, through quilting as well (c). Machine in place. Fold lace outwards and tack in place through all thicknesses (d). Fold about 7cm of this end of cocoon back on itself, quilted sides together, and tack and then machine through all thicknesses close to the broderie anglaise.

5 Fold cocoon (linings together) just less than two-thirds of way up (about 29cm). Mark with tacking stitches where the turnover comes, through lining side only.

6 Handles. Cut 21×35cm piece of quilting in half lengthwise. Fold in sides lengthwise into the middle and tack. Fold in half lengthwise, outside edges together, and machine close to edge. Machine across ends once or twice to strengthen. Repeat for second handle.

7 Pin one handle end close to top of turnover on the right side facing inwards (e) and the other end about 7cm away. Machine both handles in place, close to edge.

8 Side seams. Place quilted sides together, handles inside, lining up the turnover edge with the line of marking tacking across the back of the cocoon. Pin and tack before machining side seams of about 1cm. Turn right side out and press carefully.

Playmat/Toy Bag
Margaret Shaw, Clitheroe, Lancs

This useful playmat, which quickly converts to a toybag, will be a favourite from babyhood through the toddler years. The baby can play safely on the mat and then all toys can be collected quickly, transported and hung up tidily, inside the drawstring bag. An optional lining of waterproof fabric makes it suitable for outdoor use. At the toddler stage, the mat provides a stimulus for imaginative play.

Materials
fabric to give two circles each 2m in diameter – these circles can be patchwork or pieces of the same fabric machined together
waterproof fabric, not polythene, to give 2m diameter circle (optional)
7m tape for drawstring
sewing thread

Method

1 Cut out three circles for lining, waterproof layer, and top fabric (patchwork if desired).

2 Stitch lining to interlining round the perimeter.

3 Stitch top fabric to lining, right sides together, leaving an opening to turn.

4 Turn to right side and stitch a channel for the drawstring.

5 Insert the drawstring.

Ooloo the Owl

Susan M. W. Vaidya, Camborne, Cornwall

Ooloo can be changed at will from a shoulder bag to a stand-up cuddly toy. It weighs only 30g so is easy to post. It is 20cm wide and 16cm deep.

Materials

43×20cm honey-brown fur fabric
43×20cm orange taffeta for lining
10×5cm white fur fabric
11.5×14cm pink felt
2.5×5cm black felt
20cm Velcro 1.5cm wide
90cm gold silky cord
sewing thread to match brown fur

Method

1   From the taffeta, draw 2 tea-plate-size circles (about 18cm across) and 2 wing patterns. Cut out.
2   Repeat in brown fur fabric.
3   From the white fur, cut out the eye feathers, with pile in direction indicated by the arrow.
4   From the black felt, cut out two eye pupils.
5   From the pink felt, cut out one beak, and four feet.

Sewing Up

1   Right sides together, stitch a curved dart in the beak top. Fold wrong sides together. Using a small zig-zag stitch sew edge of beak from A to B, leaving the end open. Stuff firmly.
2   Zig-zag 2 feet together along the edge C to D, stitching up the claws to c and d. Stuff firmly. Repeat.
3   Line the 2 wings by sewing right sides together, leaving a turning gap. Turn and sew the opening.
4   Zig-zag the black pupils on to the white fur, as shown on the pattern.
5   With pile downwards, mark the bottom of each body circle, on the wrong side. Pin the white eye feather piece to the upper half of the front body, with the

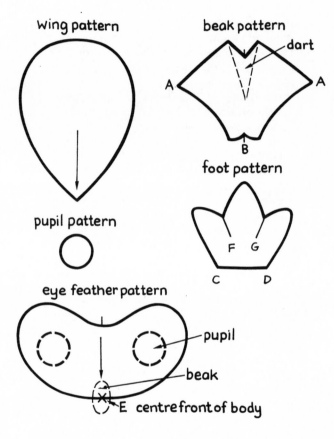

wing pattern

beak pattern

dart

A   A

B

pupil pattern

foot pattern

F   G

C   D

eye feather pattern

pupil

beak

E centre front of body

enlarge × 2

136

layout

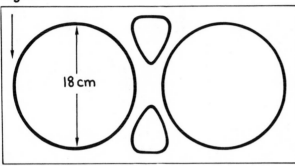

18 cm

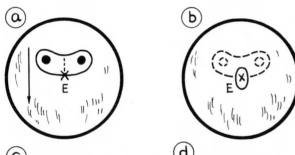

(a) E

(b) E

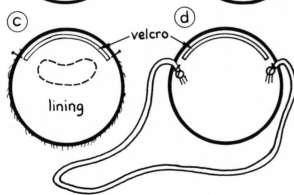

(c) velcro

lining

(d)

lowest convex part at mid-centre E. Appliqué it with zig-zag stitch, keeping the fur away from the needle with the point of a pair of scissors (a).

6 With the dart at the top, zig-zag the beak to the body over centre point E (b).

7 Line front and back bodies as in step 3.

8 Place back and front together, pile downwards. Mark the position of the top opening of the bag by placing a pair of pins at the rim of the body on the level with the top of the eye-feathers at each side. Separate. Tack about 17cm of rough Velcro to the top inside back body following the curve between the pins. Sew the Velcro inner edge first, snipping the outer edge, as necessary, to keep it close to the body edge, then sew the outer edge. Do the same on the inside front with the matching soft Velcro strip. With a needle flick loose any captured fur on the outsides (c).

9 Adjust the length of the shoulder strap. Tie a knot each end. Sew firmly to the back body, just below the Velcro (d).

10 Sew the front edge of the wings to the front body at the sides, about 1.5cm in from the edge.

11 Tack the feet to the lining at bottom of front, in line with the black pupils.

12 Pin the wings forward. Fasten the Velcro. Zig-zag back and front together from the end of the Velcro, around the outside bottom of the body, enclosing the feet.

13 Open the bag. Catch the wings back with a few stitches to the back body.

14 To make Ooloo stand up, tuck the cord inside, add enough treasures to stuff the bag, close the Velcro and catch the feet forward with hidden stitches.

137

enlarge × 4

Travel Handy
Barbara E. Thorpe, Sheffield

A useful bag with pockets, suitable for any age group from babies to grannies, largely made from remnants.

Materials
remnants of cottons or similar, plain and patterned, to include:
90×30cm blue gingham for sky
90×23cm green seersucker for grass
90×53cm curtain lining or calico (will not be seen)
1m×99cm dark blue cotton or plastic for lining and pockets
23×30cm red poplin for letters
30×46cm plaid or large check for train – allow enough material to match plaid on carriages
small black oddments for people
green cottons, plain and prints, for trees 15cm deep
90×53cm 50g terelyne wadding (thin)
1m medium iron-on interfacing
22cm diameter rush table mat for base, or if preferred a piece of denim 25cm in diameter

2m red cord for drawstring
card for templates of train, trees, etc – old greetings cards are excellent
selection of sewing cottons to match fabrics. Machine embroidery thread is best for zig-zag but Sylko 50 (fine) can be used. Tacking cotton in several colours if possible. Oddments of stranded silks for daisies and grass
10 black buttons for wheels 1.5cm
tracing paper, pencil and usual sewing equipment

Method
If a swing-needle sewing machine is not available, use straight stitch and oversew with herringbone or buttonhole stitch. Iron all fabrics before sewing as quilting cannot be ironed.

To make body of bag
1 Turn in bottom edge of blue check and top edge of green seersucker 1cm and pin. Overlap green over blue, tack together and machine, making one piece 90×53cm.

2 Lay curtain lining backing on table, then 50g wadding of same size, covered by blue/green piece right side up.

3 Tack from centre outwards, through all thicknesses at 10cm intervals across and down, with white thread to hold layers firm while machining. Mark outline of panel to be appliquéd in brown tacking cotton. Design is worked flat before joining side seam.

4 Measure mat base circumference (approx 72cm), add 5cm for seam allowance. Mark area 77cm across by 46cm down with pins and tack round rectangle with brown cotton. Mark a line across top, 8cm down, to allow for seam and drawstring channel. Mark another line for bottom of panel 46cm from top, again in brown tacking. Divide working area 77×38cm through centre down and across with tacking threads as guidelines while making up. Do not cut off surplus until making up bag, as quilting can take up some fabric.

5 Using main diagram, trace off design on tissue paper. Lay over prepared fabric right side up and pin round edges to prevent movement, then using small stitches tack all round each shape taking care to mark corners clearly. Use green tacking for trees and red for train and letters, black for people so that you can easily see positions for appliqué. Tear paper off carefully leaving stitched outlines behind.

6 Using diagram, again trace off outline of each piece. Transfer to card to make templates of them all.

7 Select materials and iron on interfacing, glistening side to wrong side of material.

8 *Reverse* card template and draw round each, in pencil, on wrong side of material. Take care to get any pattern central as on train carriages.

9 Cut out each one with sharp-pointed scissors. To get clean edge on windows and letters pierce centre of fabric to be removed, slash to corners, and cut out pieces.

10 Start building up picture appliqué, trees first. Dotted lines mark overlapping of tree. Do not stitch under-parts – the top tree will hold it in place. Pin in position and tack 5mm from edges, except for trees marked A and B. These overlap seam so leave outer half of A and all of B until side is joined. Zig-zag round each with green machine embroidery cotton, stitch setting 1+2. Remove tacking. Close zig-zag is done later.

11 Tack train and people in place tucking necks under carriage tops. Using red thread, straight stitch round train close to edge then sew again in close zig-zag, stitch setting 3+½. Outline people in black thread, stitch setting 1+2, then again closer, stitch setting 2+½. Remove all tacking threads.

12 Tack letters in place starting from engine funnel to resemble smoke. Outline in red straight stitch. Remove tacking then, taking care to hold material flat, close zig-zag each letter in stitch setting 3+½.

13 Stitch buttons in position for wheels using red cotton.

14 Close zig-zag edges of trees still exposed.

Lining

1 Out of lining fabric cut main piece 77×53cm, strip for pockets 77×23cm and circle 26cm in diameter for base.

2 Cover 20m diameter card circle with wadding same size. Run a gathering thread 1cm in on fabric circle. Lay over wadding and pull tight so gathers are under card base.

3 Turn in top of pocket strip 1.5cm and machine. Use contrast thread so pockets can easily be seen.

4 Tack to right side of lining 23cm from top edge. Machine sides and bottom edge in zig-zag 1+2. Divide into 1 large, 2 medium and 1 small pockets. Zig-zag down each, finishing off firmly top and bottom. Remember seam join will divide two pockets.

5 With right sides together, lay lining (pockets inside) over body of bag, topmost edges even. Pin, tack, and machine using straight stitch, 2cm in across top of

bag. Open out and press seam flat with fingers. *Check measurement* with circumference of base mat and adjust if necessary.

6 Side seam. Fold in half, right sides in, edges matching (make sure tree A is not caught in seam). Tack and machine through bag, then lining, to form long tube. Trim seam allowance.

7 Turn right side out. Run gathering thread 1.5cm from bottom of lining to draw up later. Turn hem 4cm deep to inside of bag bottom. Tack only. Finish tree A and apply tree B over seam.

8 Fold on top seam and pull lining inside so wrong sides are together. Pin in place. Mark stitching lines for drawstring 3cm and 5.5cm from top. Machine along each to make channel for cord.

9 Embroider 2 eyelets for cord through bag fabrics only (not lining) in centre of channel 1cm either side of side seam and 1cm either side of halfway fold. Using lazy-daisy stitch and straight stitch sew a few flowers and grasses in spaces around lower trees.

10 Pulling lining down into position, tack through all thicknesses of lining and bag 3cm from bottom, matching side seams, taking care lining does not pull tight. Machine and remove tacking.

Base 1 (using rush mat)

1 Using matching double thread and a strong needle, oversew outside of bag to edge of rush mat. Check lining bottom is tucked away inside as this lies over top of mat when finished. Insert needle between rows of mat using small stitches and fasten off securely.

2 Draw up gathering thread in lining to lie flat over mat base. Place ready-made lining base over to cover raw edges. Push down firmly. Knot through both base and mat, tying on inside, one in centre and four round outer edge. Leave 1cm-long ends. To save weakening rush mat see that thread passes either side of row, not through a row.

3 Cut 2m red cord in half and thread each through eyelets in channel round top of bag, joining with a knot to make a circle, one on each side of bag. Bind ends for 1.5cm and fray out to make a tassel on each side. Pull to draw up.

Base 2 (using denim and card)

Do not turn up bottom of bag as in base 1.

1 Make a base of strong card 21cm in diameter and denim circle 25cm in diameter. Turn bag inside out. With right sides together tack bag and lining as one to denim base, easing round circle. Machine stitch twice, taking 4cm seam allowance. Trim outside to 3cm leaving lining 4cm.

2 Turn to right side. Push out bottom firmly, checking outer edge is fully stretched.

3 Lay strong card under seam allowance. Run gathering thread through all thicknesses of material and pull up to lie flat on card.

4 Place ready-made inner base over to cover raw edges and press down. Stitch lightly round edge of base to lining.